Praise for Recovery Hardware

Recovery Hardware is all about taking that leap of faith in others. Gina Schaefer has kicked down doors in a field long dominated by men, so she can share a new way of doing business. She turns the spotlight on trusting those in recovery, to take a company beyond just numbers. Recovery Hardware is brilliant and brave, heartbreaking and uplifting. There is so much to learn from this story.

—ROBERT HOHMAN, CHAIRMAN AND CO-FOUNDER OF GLASSDOOR

Recovery Hardware is a story about grit and a big heart against all odds. How does a person with no retail experience and no hardware knowledge succeed? Gina is a woman in a man's playground teaching us all a different way to sell hardware. A wonderful, compelling read for any entrepreneur who has a soul and a passion to win while leaving the world a better place.

—RAY A. GRIFFITH RETIRED PRESIDENT/CEO ACE HARDWARE CORPORATION.

If you've never thought to look in the plumbing aisle or gardening department for stories of redemption and the healing power of connection, this book will forever change your sense of what locally owned, brick-and-mortar businesses do for their communities. With humor and insight, Schaefer offers a deeply engaging memoir of building a business that meets the restoration needs of its neighbors in ways both practical and metaphysical.

Business leaders often say "our people are our most important asset." The story of Recovery Hardware certainly demonstrates the importance of employees to the success of the enterprise, but it also reveals the wisdom of Gina Schaefer in not viewing employees as assets, but rather seeing them as whole people – people with their own blend of strengths and frailties, aspirations and fears, and yearnings for connection and control over their lives. Recovery Hardware recounts the joy of building a business that contributes to the well-being of people and the health of communities, as well as the heartbreak of inevitably finding the limitations of the business' ability to fix what is broken. In this time of economic polarization, surveillance, and mistrust, it is uplifting to read about a business built on trust in people and a commitment to community.

Recovery Hardware is the inspiring true story of a passionate young woman who sets out to leave the rat race of corporate America and act on her lifelong dream of being an entrepreneur but along the way creates a community where those recovering from addiction find a place of refuge. Through her moving re-telling of "heartware" stories, author Gina Schaefer emphasizes the idea that we can all learn something from everyone we meet, just as she has through her interactions with her team members from all walks of life. In the words of Schaefer – "There is only one way to grow life and that is to understand and empathize with the experiences of others". Filled with life lessons not just for her fellow entrepreneurs and business owners but everyone with a heart, this is truly one of those books you will read more than once and gift to others!

Don`t expect this to be a story of how a company was formed or how a series of hardware stores were opened, it is so much more that. This is a story of how people`s lives have come together and told through the lens of an inspirational founder who just happened to believe in the goodness of people and the value of giving that goodness some space to shine.

Gina Schaefer is the quintessential social entrepreneur. Through her unrelenting drive and passion for social justice and equitable business practices she has founded an enviable business model. One that does well while doing good.

The vignettes Gina Schaefer shares are intensely personal and human and perfectly mirror the experience of walking into any one of her stores. What Gina has created is a powerful social enterprise, with positive social change baked into the DNA of the company.

Gina reached into the corporate toolbox and, like any savvy consumer, chose carefully. As a thoughtful entrepreneur, she led with empathy and put people and neighborhoods at the center of her business model. With her rich storytelling, Gina reminds us that local business can not only create robust economies, but they can also change lives. Corporations can recover, too. Like Gina, they can do so with an eye toward impact and profit at once. Gina has been leading the way and with this book, others will follow.

As Gina shows so beautifully in her book, the best businesses have heart. They are communities within communities, where mutual respect and teamwork aren't just slogans. They're key to building a thriving business where people want to work and people want to shop. Gina is a great storyteller and inspiring advocate for people-centered business.

Ace always shines brightest in the darkest hour. Recovery Hardware is an endearing story of how one of thousands of Ace owners have used their business success as a springboard to be significant in the communities they serve.

Seeing Gina and team grow over the years has been amazing. This book opened my eyes to her wider team and the impact they have made on A Few Cool Hardware Stores. Gina's dedication to her communities, employees, and customers is clearly her superpower. Her focus is a great example of how entrepreneurs can be caring, nimble, unique, and successful.

—CASEY FANNON, CEO & PRESIDENT NATIONAL COOPERATIVE BANK

Gina Schaefer shares stories of resiliency that should resonate with so many people. As a business leader who has created a workplace of hope and stability, she ensures that people can believe in and live up to their full potential.

-KARA TEEPLE, MSW, CEO AND NON-PROFIT LEADER, LAWRENCE HALL, CHICAGO, IL

Gina Schaefer shares in this amazing book why family businesses are the heart of America. It is a story of how one local entrepreneur truly changed the lives of people, and an incredible example of capitalism with a conscience. A great read that will touch your heart and mind.

-HOWARD BRODSKY, FOUNDER AND CHAIRMAN OF CCA GLOBAL PARTNERS

Hardware Recovery proves that small and mid-market businesses can be one of the biggest agents for change in our world. If it's possible to grow a successful business with people in recovery, think of all the other opportunities for change there are if a company doesn't only focus on its profits. A company with a soul – who focuses on its people and stakeholders – can be one of the best ways to change someone's life while making money.

—RYAN TANSOM, CO-FOUNDER AT ARKONA AND HOST OF THE INTENTIONAL GROWTH™ PODCAST

I absolutely love this book; I was completely heart-stricken living in your pages! Beautiful. I am incredibly curious like an anxious child to investigate the creative uniqueness of your stores. The inspiring way you write and support human creation is phenomenal. I truly hope that this book will inspire more employers to consider employees who desire second chances. Most of humanity have needed a second chance and are driven, grateful and make the best employees. You have shown us all how to build relationships and make our world a more inclusive place, full of love and examples of kindness.

—CHRISTI POWELL, WOMEN BUSINESS ENTERPRISE, 84 LUMBER COMPANY

RECOVERY HARDWARE

A Nuts-and-Bolts Story About Building a Business, Restoring a Community and Renovating Lives

Contact information for Persistently Local Publishing– www.recoveryhardware.com

ISBN: 979-8-9858410-0-8 (paperback)
ISBN: 979-8-9858410-2-2 (hardback)
ISBN: 979-8-9858410-1-5 (ebook)

Ordering Information:
Special discounts are available on quantity purchases by corporations, associations, and others.
For details, contact the author through www.recoveryhardware.com

Cover artwork by Gil Roeder gil.roeder@gmail.com

RECOVERY HARDWARE

A Nuts-and-Bolts Story About Building
a Business, Restoring a Community
and Renovating Lives

Gina Schaefer

Dedication

To Whitman -Walker Addiction Services, whose clients crossed the street to our little shop, giving me the gift of the best teammates in the world.

To my beloved neighborhood, Logan Circle—what it was and what it has become—and to all the communities that support us. We see all those hammers and snow shovels and plungers you've purchased and appreciate you.

"I always wondered why someone doesn't do something about that. Then I realized that I was somebody."

—*Unknown*

Contents

You're Not a Clone, Why Shop at One?

f it's different or unique, I'm drawn to it—that's why all our hardware stores develop their own style and why I love each and every one. They are all quirky and special in their own way and that's by design. We want every store to reflect the spirit of the people who shop and work there, and to honor the unique demands of our neighborhoods.

But if truth were told, I do have one favorite spot. It's the lawn and garden department at Logan Hardware, in Logan Circle, our flagship community where I go to work every day. I love this little nook because it's tucked away like a secret. It's on the second floor, way at the back so you can easily miss it. In fact, you almost have to will yourself to find it. But once you do, it's a like a gift of sensory overload in the most beautiful and unexpected of ways.

There are hundreds of colorful flowerpots here, of all shapes and sizes, glass vessels and kitschy floor mats, cacti and wind chimes. Old wooden pallets hang from the ceiling to make more space for macrame plant hangers and vividly hued watering cans. Right around the corner from the explosion of houseplants is a small set of stairs that lead to what was once a carriage house. This hidden space smells like a true old-fashioned hardware store—the dirt and fertilizer and bird seed of generations gone by perfumes the air.

To top it all off, hanging two stories above the alley, there is a back deck that teems with gorgeous plants basking in the city sunshine for as long as the season allows. It doesn't matter that the deck is not at ground level and overlooks an urban alley. Those details fade away when you step out and become enveloped in the bright blooms. In our busier seasons you can barely fit through the aisles of plant carts we have jammed back there. We cram as much variety as possible into about 300 square feet, so our city-dwelling neighbors feel like they have escaped to the countryside.

There is a back stairwell that links the third-floor offices where I spend most of my day to this bucolic retail nook. I sneak away to spend time there whenever I get stressed or bored or claustrophobic. It refreshes my perspective and reminds me of why I'm running a retail business in the first place. It's because of nooks like this, brimming over with rare beauty, that you can smell, touch, and see. It's because I have built places like this all over town, where even the most delicate of flowers and people can grow and bloom.

In writing this book, I've come to realize that my life has been punctuated by a strong connection to places—places like the garden department I just described. From a tiny business set up in my childhood basement to communities throughout the DC and Baltimore metro areas, I set down roots, and then I provide a place where others hopefully can feel at home. I build places where communities can come together, and take care of themselves, and each other. That after all, is what a hardware store should be about.

Quite coincidentally, our inaugural store opened down the block from The Elizabeth Taylor Medical Center, which has a successful drug addiction recovery program under its umbrella. From the very first person who drifted across the street to ask for work, I have been impressed with the quality, determination, and grace of my employees in recovery. From them I have learned patience and tolerance, discipline and forgiveness, leadership and fellowship, determination, and grace.

When one of my teammates stood in front of me one day and said to me, "You know, Gina, we are known as *recovery hardware* in the community," the reason to write this book took hold. This book is an opportunity for me to lift up the men and women in recovery who have taught me how to be a leader, how to be a neighbor, and how to be a true friend. I have grown alongside them for almost two decades and my path would not have been nearly as fun or fulfilling or as successful without them. I like to think that it led to my own growth and recovery as a person with a voice, and as a leader who does the right thing. And ultimately, I believe that the collective efforts at our stores have led to the growth and recovery of our neighborhoods, and our communities.

3

Over the years the word recovery has meant different things at different times to different people. For me, what began as an effort to help my community recover from decades of neglect morphed into helping dozens (and dozens) of folks in recovery find a place where they could be safe from judgement, learn to show up on time, and give it their all. I wanted to share with them my sense of place where they could build a happy and fulfilling life.

I've met so many special people because I am the owner of a retail business and want to tell some of their stories. I hope you hear their voices as their stories unfold, and that you find them as inspiring and helpful to you as they were to me.

Come on in.

ONE

If You Are Quiet, You Can Hear the Future Whispering

Everything around me was wonderfully quiet. Calm. Hushed in a way that most twelve-year-olds don't usually appreciate. There were so few times during the day when I was even halfway still—sitting peacefully without my mind or my mouth running a hundred miles an hour. So, I relished this unusual and precious silence. It was as if my whole being was sitting inside noise-canceling headphones—those big bulbous cans that cover your entire ear—except this silence surrounded my head and enveloped my shoulders too.

I could hear my own steady breathing: deep breath in, shmmmmmm; then a long breath out, mmmmmm. Shmmmmmm. Mmmmmmm.

I could just faintly make out every other letter in the words my mom was yelling from the kitchen upstairs: "s....s....t...me..... to.....ge.....moooov.....ng!" *Sis, time to get moving!*

I knew what she was saying even if the soothing silence under my electric shroud was drowning out her voice. I knew, because I had been sitting under the same old-style hairdryer, cross-legged, and cozy every single weekday morning for as long as I could remember. Every day, we went through the same routine.

On this particular day, I was putting the finishing touches on my first business plan and wanted every last second of prep time I could get before I had to run and catch the bus to elementary school. My best friend and I had decided to start an after-school daycare program for little kids and I was finishing the financial projections. I needed to document that we were going to charge a nickel for a carton of milk. Milk and cookies would be our upsell.

Even back then, I knew that I wanted to own my own business. It was as if I sensed that I would be a terrible employee, so I prepared to be my own boss early to get a jump on the game. I had already started babysitting. From there, I figured that if I could earn one dollar an hour taking care of one child, imagine the buckets of money I could make if I watched the whole neighborhood at the same time!

My fledgling daycare dream never got off the ground, but I will never forget the work I put into scheming and drafting and researching it. I filled a ruled notebook with ideas and fees and strategies—snippets of things I had read about on my nearly daily visits to the town library. My notes were written in big loopy flourishes and on some pages, I had used colored pencils for emphasis. I was serious.

My memories from those days mostly hinge on the enthusiasm and empowerment I felt, blissfully unaware of the countless obstacles girls face when it comes to doing just about anything. Years later, when people started to ask me why I decided to open a chain of hardware stores, I thought back to these memories. I thought back to the joy of planning that daycare center and realized that it was those plans that helped lead me to where I am today. I also think back to the important lessons I learned from my hard-working dad, and my entrepreneurial mom.

My dad worked two full-time jobs for 25 years. He worked on an assembly line for the Hoover Company, and he drove a school bus for our small town. Depending on how you orient a day, he went to his first job at 10:00 p.m., and his second one at 7:00 a.m. AND 3:00 p.m. In between, he slept. I'm exhausted just thinking about it. If that doesn't create a foundation for hard work as a way of life, I don't know what does. My dad taught me punctuality, time management, and a bit of thriftiness. Traits that I now know are not easy to come by and can't be taught in an orientation session or online business class.

My enterprising mother opened her own hair salon a.k.a. a *beauty shop* in our tiny Ohio basement. It had a linoleum floor and smelled like peroxide. The room wasn't very big, maybe twelve feet wide by twelve deep, but when you're young everything looms large, and the beauty shop seemed cavernous. As you entered from the garage, you could peer into our kitchen with its Brady Bunch-style orange countertops and a view down to the crick (or "creek" for non-Ohioans). No one had to step into the kitchen to get to the shop but there were lots of customers always passing by. There were 12 stairs carpeted in shaggy green and flanked with brown-paneled walls that led the way to the space below.

Many of my mom's clients were older women who came each week to spend time chatting with anyone who would listen. Topics generally included cranky husbands and *Days of Our Lives.* Grown children who wouldn't visit or grandkids who were cute as a button also ranked high on the list. My mom's ladies wanted pin curls or blue hair rinses and they would sleep upright for six nights with their hair wrapped in toilet paper and hairnets until they came back again for a refresh.

I was my mom's best and only hair model basically from the time I had hair. Most teenagers are absolutely terrified of having the wrong hair or wrong clothes—hell, so are most adults—but my hair was a daily science experiment, and I didn't care. I spent hours and hours in that shop with those ladies and my mom with her scissors and chemicals and curlers. If Mom wanted to see what I looked like with a perm, I showed up at school with curls. If she wanted to try out a new haircut she saw in a magazine, I might wind up with bangs.

"It's cute!" or "It'll grow back, I promise," she would say if I started to tug at the fringe or looked the slightest bit panicked.

My grandmother was one of our weekly visitors and there was no place for tears in my grandma's world. "Straighten up, the curls will come out," she'd admonish me. I would turn my head to the right, and then the left, peering into mirror, trying to convince myself that whatever my mom had just done to my thick brown locks was *just fine.* All of this explains childhood photos where I *sort of* looked like Dorothy Hamill or I *sort of* looked like Princess Leia. Both of my parents believe that if you can't say anything nice, don't say anything at all, so I learned to keep my mouth shut, and just rolled with it because in time, I knew I'd get a do-over anyway—hair or otherwise.

My absolute favorite part of having a beauty shop in my house was sitting under the hairdryer and tuning out the world while I planned and plotted in my own private think tank.

The chair was a 1970s-inspired harvest gold. A sickly mustardy-looking thing that should have gone out of style and stayed there. The large, clear plastic hood that lowered over your head was dotted with tiny venting holes and had a square neck connecting it to the chair. Once lowered, the dome hovered over your head and the hot air circulated and dried your locks without blowing them around. To me, it was nirvana.

The chair's seat was wide and encased in a thick, sticky plastic. Before lowering myself onto the seat, I would put down a fluffy bath towel so I wouldn't become permanently adhered to it, imprinting angry red marks on my legs. I loved that dryer and those morning moments more than anything in my life up until that point. There have been stressful periods in my adult life when I have longed to have that morning ritual back—to have an hour of solitude in a noiseless world.

My mom and her courageous tonsorial experimentation taught me how to move on and move through challenges—hair grows back, styles change—and there's nothing that's going to happen that I can't look at straight in the mirror and work out. My dad taught me about hard work, and about the good feeling that you get at the end of the day when you have worked for something larger than yourself. My grandmother taught me that complaining doesn't get you anywhere, and that there's nothing that a little time and a resilient spirit can't fix. There, in that harvest-gold chair with my hair in braids or bangs or a brand-new permanent, absorbing the lessons in business and life that surrounded me every day, is where my story began. It was in that white noise, alone in that silence, that I heard my future whispering to me for the very first time. So, my advice to all aspiring empire builders is to find a little time alone in the silence, to hear yourself think.

TWO

You Never Know What Can Happen When You Lose Your Job

was alone in my little car, zipping down the GW Parkway at 6 p.m. on a Thursday evening. It was 2002. The Potomac River to my left shimmered russet and gold in the sunset and I could see the stately buildings on the Georgetown University campus off in the distance. I might have been wondering in that moment where my own education had gotten me, which at that time was precisely nowhere. The conversation I had just had in my office was still spinning in my head as I switched over to the travel lane and drifted my way from the suburbs toward my home in the city.

"Sorry, we have to lay you off," the General Counsel at my company had said to me unexpectedly that afternoon.

"How is that possible?" I asked. "We just got five million dollars in funding. How can you lay me off now?"

"Sorry, Gina, we spent it all. It's gone. We're done. You're done. There is nothing left."

"Who is going to tell the investors?" I asked him, stunned that this guy and not my boss was telling me I was being let go.

"You are going to tell them, Gina," the GC told me, matter-of-factly. "That's your last assignment. Call everybody, tell them their money is gone, and tell them you're really sorry."

I'm sorry? Me? This wasn't my fault. Of course, the GC knew that, but just as it hadn't been the CEO's job to talk to me, it wasn't the General Counsel's job to tell the investors. It was mine.

I couldn't believe this was happening to me *again*. To be fair, I wasn't completely shocked. I had been in this uncomfortable situation twice in two years. The tech boom and bust racket was brutal and I was starting to feel a little beat up by the whole thing.

This is when I started thinking back to the business plan I had created at 12 years old on my mom's sticky salon chair. Ever since then, I had wanted to own my own business but could never quite figure out what type of business I wanted to start. I didn't want to start a beauty shop like my mom and I definitely did not want to start a tech company. My dreams of babysitting glory were behind me. So, what then? I didn't have an answer. As a result, I kept hitching my star to someone else's wagon, and the damn wagons kept crashing.

One thing I knew for sure, I was sick of driving out of the city. My daily trek to the suburbs of Washington, DC was long and truthfully, I couldn't stand driving. Whatever I decided, I knew it was going to happen inside the city limits. I wanted to walk to work.

My conversation with the now former GC began playing in my brain on a loop. I drove home for what I hoped would be the last time, constructing what I was going to tell my husband Marc. We had just bought a new home. How was he going to react to this news?

I burst through the front door with so much energy I shook the pictures on the wall.

"Marc!" I yelled down the hallway. "I am done with commuting, and I am definitely done working for all of these stupid men!" I am about as subtle as a two by four sometimes.

There was a long moment of silence before Marc spoke.

"Okay then," said my very agreeable husband, pouring himself a drink. "How do you plan on keeping yourself busy?" He asked me this first, instead of saying something like, "That sounds fine, darling, but how are you going to earn a living?" I think he knew I would always find a way to earn a living. I was perfectly employable. But it was guaranteed that I would drive him completely crazy if I didn't figure out a way to keep myself busy.

And then I made an announcement, which seemed to him to come out of nowhere. The idea had taken hold of me on my drive home and since the moment that lightbulb had gone off, my excitement and sense of certainty grew. Inside of five minutes, I was surer of this plan than I had been about anything in a very long time.

"I am going to open a hardware store. Right here in Logan Circle," I said, as if it was the most obvious choice in the world for me, which it most certainly was not.

I knew absolutely nothing about hardware, or retail. I hadn't grown up with a hammer in my hand or with parents who taught me the ins and outs of home improvement. My one fleeting encounter with a retail career had been a two-month stint while on break from college, selling cheap jewelry in a mall shop. "I don't care what you do, just so long as you're happy," Marc said. See why I married him? Marc knew I could do anything I set my mind to, and his lack of a freak out reminded me that I knew that too. He did ask me if I was smoking crack, and then laughed and gave me a big hug. If he had any serious misgivings, he didn't express them. He was, as he always is, reliably and wonderfully supportive.

❋❋❋❋❋❋

Public service has always been a part of the vision I have for myself. The year I arrived at Wittenberg University as an undergrad, my new school had become the fifth in the country to mandate community service as a graduation requirement. The new program's Director was a dynamo named Deborah Dillon who hired me to motivate my fellow students to get their service credits done. You want to talk about push back? That was the real deal, and somehow Deb knew I was the right girl for the job.

Once a month I had a standing date in the science auditorium lecturing the football team about why they had to get off the field and into the real world. I would stand at the base of that cavernous room, the stadium seats ascending into the sky from where I stood. The higher they went, the smaller I felt. I was just this tiny freshman, telling guys four times my size to do their service because it would make them better people. Sometimes they laughed at me, often they just ignored me, but occasionally, my pep talk worked, and I got to watch some of those oversized personalities shine in a whole new way.

One particularly bright memory I have is watching a six-foot, five-inch free safety dance with seven-year-olds in a self-esteem class at a local elementary school. I will never forget the look of joy and surprise on that football player's face. I think he got more out of it than the kids. I got a lot out of it too. For those four years I developed a stronger sense of right and wrong and started to dream about a bigger life in a bigger city. I continued my commitment to service for a few years after graduation, working for the Children's Defense Fund in Washington, DC before spending a life-changing 10 months in Brazil and then somehow wound up in software.

During this time, I worked for a whole host of startups that all followed a similar path. An entrepreneur would get VC funding and think they were going to become the next Google. They would spend all that money, typically as fast as it came in, and immediately start going out of business. I would get hired and then get laid off. Rinse and repeat. Over and over again I held myself back from going for what I really wanted, which was to open my own business.

National Groups for Retailers Making a Difference

Over the years, we have gotten involved with several national organizations whose work on behalf of small businesses makes a difference every day. I would encourage anyone to check them out.

- The Institute for Local Self-Reliance
  ILSR.org
- Main Street America
  mainstreet.org
- American Independent Business Alliance
  amiba.net
- American Booksellers Association
  bookweb.org

Looking for yet another job in the tech world seemed exhausting and pointless. Plus, I loved my new neighborhood. I wanted to stay there for a while, because even though Logan Circle had seen better days, it was, much like myself at that time, in search of a new path to glory.

Once a bustling hub of industry and entertainment, Logan Circle was destroyed during the 1968 riots that broke out the day that Martin Luther King Jr. was assassinated.[1] As the news of King's death spread from Tennessee northward, crowds began to gather at the intersection of 14th and U Streets just three blocks from where my office sits today. The real disturbance began when a window was broken at the People's Drug Store.[2] The looters then spread throughout the neighborhood, block by block, tearing everything down as they went.

By the time peace was finally restored, 200 stores had had their windows broken, 150 others had been looted,[3] 13 people had been killed[4] and over a thousand people had been injured.[5] For the next three decades, Logan Circle sat there, untouched and unloved. When you walked around the neighborhood back then, and even now, you could feel the ghosts.

Despite all of this, or maybe even because of it, my husband Marc and I fell in love with the place.

We got involved with the Logan Circle Community Association (LCCA) as soon as we moved in. We started to make some friends who were also, like us, trying to reclaim the streets. The grit didn't bother us because the coming change was palpable. We could literally feel the ground swell—Logan Circle was on its way up. The LGBTQ+ community had started moving east, out of hipper Dupont Circle, in search of cheaper housing, and they were running smack dab into our neighborhood.

A circular park, complete with a namesake statute of an antique war hero, ran through the center of the community. No one used the park; it was litter strewn and punctuated by patchy sections of grass and the occasional discarded crack vial. Neighbors didn't even want to walk their dogs there for fear of them stepping on needles or swallowing the chicken bones that dotted the sidewalks.

The park itself was surrounded by the faded elegance of row houses in all sizes and colors, just begging for new owners to love them again. Not far away, an abandoned commercial corridor screamed with potential. Everything the eye could see was ripe for restoration.

Soon, new neighbors, all urban pioneers just like us, were moving into the boarded-up buildings and preparing for long months of rehab. They bought their houses for a song and went to work restoring them to period or creating more contemporary versions that nevertheless still expressed their former glory. Before our eyes, our battered 'hood was being transformed into a picture of optimism and creative recovery.

I had, in fact, given the idea of a hardware store quite a lot of thought. It wasn't a totally hair-brained idea. As active members of the LCCA, we knew our neighbors all wanted to see the same kinds of places open in the neighborhood. They wanted the fundamentals: a grocery store, a pharmacy, a health clinic, better schools, and yes, you guessed it, a hardware store.

Out of those essential options, hardware was the only one that spoke to me, maybe because it was the opposite of software, or maybe it was because I was surrounded by houses in various stages of restoration, all crying out for one thing—hardware! Whatever it was, suddenly I knew what I wanted to do. I started to research the industry and discovered that a hardware store, crazy as it sounded, wasn't a bad business model for me.

At that time, there were three large national purchasing cooperatives for independent hardware stores and of those three, Ace Hardware responded to our inquiries first. I liked the feel of this organic, small-business-led growth, and I shared their midwestern values of power through collective effort. For me, Ace sounded like it really was the place.

The Birth of the Co-op

Ace Hardware was founded in 1924 in Chicago, Illinois when a small group of entrepreneurs joined forces to get better pricing from their vendors.[6] Working from a truly cooperative principle, they knew they were better and stronger together and the group grew from there. They told a friend, who told a friend, until eventually there were thousands of locally owned Ace Hardware stores all over the country. They named their company Ace after the Flying Aces, the famous World War I fighter pilots known the world over for their bravery, resilience, and ability to overcome all odds.[7]

Cooperatives are like secret weapons for small business owners. Ace helps us aggregate purchasing, training, and services so that we can compete against bigger, better-funded retailers every day. I've made friends all over the country who I can call for advice and support when the need arises.

Ace sent Richard Mann, their local Business Development Manager, to see me, ostensibly to help guide me through the process of becoming a retailer. I didn't know it at the time, but he was really there to turn down my application. They just didn't see how a hardware store in a city like Washington, DC could ever be successful.

Maybe I'm rewriting history, but at the time, it seemed like Richard really did understand my vision for a locally owned store in a rebounding urban neighborhood like ours. I thought he sympathized with my desire to help this community recover. I imagined that he saw, like I did, the possibilities in this tiny slice of city life, just begging to be loved after years of needless neglect.

Really Big Companies You may not have Known were Cooperatives

- Cabot Creamery
- REI
- Land-o-Lakes
- Ocean Spray
- Sunkist Growers Inc.
- Welch Foods Inc.

There are seven cooperative principles:

- Voluntary and open membership
- Democratic member control
- Members' economic participation
- Autonomy and independence
- Education, training and information
- Cooperation among cooperatives
- Concern for community[8]

All you had to do was stand on any corner and look up and down

14th Street to see how great Logan Circle was about to become. You could see men in hard hats circling vacant lots. Every day some news source was reporting a potential new development or business about to open. It never crossed my mind that Richard had his eye on a different opportunity, one that had nothing to do with reclaiming my neighborhood, and everything to do with the big commission he got for landing a new co-op member.

Richard appeared to sign off on me, and I was overjoyed. He told me to go ahead and find a commercial space, sign a 10-year lease, then fax a copy of that lease along with my completed application back to the Ace headquarters in Oak Brook, Illinois. He'd take care of the rest.

So, I went location shopping. There wasn't exactly a cornucopia of ripe retail spaces for rent in the community. In fact, there was really just one place that was ready, although the word *ready* was a misnomer. The space had broken-out windows and two inches of pigeon droppings on the second floor. It was dark, smelled terrible and you had to have serious vision and optimism to get past your initial reaction, which was a great big gulp of multi-sensory yuck.

Nonetheless, everyone in Logan Circle trying to open a business at that time had set their sights on this dilapidated shell of a pseudo-corner lot, which was owned by a local developer named Jim. All eyes were on Jim and his property because a CVS had opened next door and just next to that was a brand spanking new Fresh Fields grocery store. The opening of Fresh Fields heralded a new level of gentrification in the area. It was the biggest thing since the World's Fair in those parts, so competition was fierce to be next door to those pricey, upscale farm-to-table aisles.

The neighborhood had lobbied Fresh Fields to open a location in Logan Circle for years. On top of phone campaigns, we had waged letter-writing wars—both to the city for help in our efforts and to the executives at Fresh Fields themselves. We were all tired of traveling distances for healthy food. The existing grocery store stunk, we weren't actually sure how old the food was or where it had come from. When the Fresh Fields finally opened, the community heaved a huge sigh of relief.

If there was a neighborhood worksheet, we could now check the box next to "supermarket." We could walk our dog and get a piece of fruit on the same trip. Imagine such luxury and convenience! And that fruit would no doubt be organic, responsibly sourced, and reflective of the new demographic in town. In return, the neighborhood patronized the store like it was their job. That location became the highest grossing unit in the Fresh Fields chain for a few years running.

I knew it was an outside shot that I'd be the lucky candidate that got the lease for that coveted lot next to Fresh Fields, but I figured if I didn't start asking for what I wanted, how would I ever get what I needed? The very next day, I marched into Jim's office with my business plan, a big smile, and a staunch resolve not to take no for an answer.

The meeting took place in his office at a low wooden table, with a paper mountain of business plans from other applicants stacked prominently and strategically in the center of that tiny tabletop. If it was a play to intimidate me, it worked. His operation seemed so sophisticated compared to whatever modicum of professionalism I had mustered for the meeting. It felt hopeless.

It wasn't long, though, before Jim and I discovered quite miraculously that we were both from the same part of Ohio. For two small-town souls, managing to find each other on a street corner in DC, it was meaningful and portentous. We bonded instantly. Beyond our Ohio connection, I knew that Jim knew how much the neighborhood wanted a hardware store and I also knew that he wanted to be the guy to give it to them. He was the right developer at the right time in the right building for me, and all I had to do was to let him be the hero. That sounded like a win/win to me. By the time I left, I had secured a 10-year lease.

And that is how, in June 2002, mere months after getting laid off from my third job, I signed an almost two-million-dollar lease for my first hardware store at 14th and P Street. I spent the next hour and a half faxing dozens of signed sheets of paper off to the Ace corporate headquarters in Oak Brook, just like Richard had told me to do, giddy the entire time. Then I waited for Richard to work his magic.

Unfortunately, mere seconds later, the General Counsel for Ace called me, and it wasn't to say welcome to the family. From that point forward, things started to go sideways quick. The Ace lawyer explained that Richard had told me to do things backwards. I was supposed to get approval from Ace BEFORE I signed a 10-year lease, not after, and as it turned out, they didn't want to approve me at all. It seemed pretty clear that Richard had told me to sign the lease first on purpose. If I had done it the right way, Ace might very well have rejected me on the spot.

As I was to learn later, Ace didn't believe a woman could open a hardware store at all, let alone in some decaying urban enclave, and make a go of it. But thanks to Richard's greed and duplicity, Ace was stuck with me. I had signed a legally binding agreement, and I wasn't going anywhere. Richard was fired that day, and Ace store #11410 was born. Logan Hardware and I were forging a new path, and all because I had lost my job, and stumbled backwards into a new adventure.

THREE

Unchecking the Boxes

Now that I had taken the leap and become a real live entrepreneur, I realized I also had to become an employer or in other words, a boss. This seemed pretty easy when I was just bossing around Marc and our friends, who all graciously volunteered for shifts while I was preparing for opening day. They donated hours and hours of their time, helping me to hang shelves and stock products and all without compensation or even lighting and heat for that matter. But one of my first full-fledged, not-related-to-me employees who actually did get a paycheck was a returning citizen named Tommy, who taught me an awful lot about the responsibilities of leadership.

Tommy was the first "ex-con" I had ever met—years before the phrase returning citizen was part of my vocabulary. We weren't sure of the details of and reason for his incarceration since we didn't put a "prior felony convictions" box on our employment application. We didn't want to rule people out through such a checklist because who knew who might walk into your life with that obstacle removed.

But just by watching and talking with him and putting two and two together, we figured out that Tommy had been locked up for about 17 years. Although who knows if he really *did* anything to deserve it. The system has never been kind to young Black men, especially in the inner city.

All I knew was that Tommy worked hard, and he was incredibly likeable. He just needed a job in a place where he could be himself, where his past didn't matter and he could carry on where he left off, but better—recovered somehow. A hardware store seemed like a good place to make that happen and I could give that to him.

In exchange, Tommy appointed himself as my personal protector. Marc would drop me off in front of the hardware store most mornings as he started his workday commute. Tommy would already be there, a big grin on his face, leaning on whatever bike he was riding that day, waiting for us.

"Morning, Marc!" Tommy would say with a wave of his hand that told my husband, *Don't worry, I've got her from here.* It made Marc feel more comfortable, this unofficial bodyguard of mine— even though neither of us ever felt unsafe in our neighborhood. It was nice to know there was another person in the store who cared about me and had my back.

Tommy was surprisingly great with our customers. He was that rare person who could talk to anyone—he treated everyone exactly the same way. He could just as easily chat up the young guys at the barbershop next door as an elderly customer or a new community member straight out of Georgetown. He also introduced us to the old-school landmarks of our hood, like the greasy breakfast joint around the corner where you could get the best fried egg sandwich on white bread with home fries for $1.99. He had breakfast there every morning, and when I could spare the time, I would join him, cholesterol be damned.

There was an older Asian lady who ran the counter, and she and Tommy went at it like an old married couple. Honestly, I was never sure whether they liked each other or hated each other, but they depended on one another for this daily dance, whatever it meant, to give shape and meaning to their morning routine. Tommy and that diner and those delicious greasy egg sandwiches were our link to a Logan Circle that was rapidly disappearing. I wanted to stay connected to this part of Logan Circle. It was an integral part of what made the neighborhood and our store special.

I have always been growth and future oriented. I love seeing new things spring up through the ground, but I also wanted to preserve the flavor of the old Logan Circle. I always wanted to be able to grab a $1.99 egg sandwich for breakfast with Tommy, or a cheap drink at Playbill during happy hour. I wanted to remember where we had come back from, and what this neighborhood still was, deep down in its soul.

Logan Circle is adjacent to U Street, which, way before my time, was known as "Black Broadway."[9] On any given night, you could hear artists like Pearl Bailey, Louis Armstrong, or Billie Holiday making music and history. Duke Ellington was born in the neighborhood.[10] Madame Lillian Evanti, the first African American international opera star, rose to fame on U Street.[11] The list went on and on. The all-stars of Black history were shining from every crumbling nook and cranny in Logan Circle.

Ann, who had recommended Tommy, had been right about him. He was a hard worker and became an integral part of our team, helping to catch shoplifters before they left the store, unloading delivery trucks and cheerfully putting products away. It's difficult now to imagine how we would ever have made it through those first exhausting years without him.

Tommy worked on the second floor, and I worked downstairs on the main floor.

"Hey Tommy, there's a guy coming up for a screw," I'd yell up the stairs when a customer was on their way. Then Tommy would laugh so loud I could hear him on the other side of the store. Long after we had implemented the use of walkie-talkies, I'd still yell up the stairwell to Tommy and try to make him laugh.

"Why you makin' yourself carry around that big radio if you just keep yellin' all the time?" He'd shout back and laugh even louder. Even though he is long gone from our store now, I can still hear Tommy's giggles tumbling down the stairwell.

Everyone seemed smarter than me in those days but none of us really knew what we were doing and to be honest, it didn't really matter. What was important to us was that we were all giving it our best shot. Like the game show *Who Wants to Be a Millionaire*, we were mastering the use of our lifelines—calling a product's manufacturer, asking a real-life contractor or using Google became the keys to mastery, or at least, what passed as mastery for our customers.

Our feeling was (and is) that people don't have to *be* professionals to work in the hardware store—we must just all be *professional* and there is a difference. We are not performing brain surgery, we are selling products and providing good customer service, which was sorely lacking in the District of Columbia at that time. It didn't matter if you had been in jail or wouldn't have initially known what a Phillips-head screwdriver was if it hit you on the nose—if you could show up on time, help the customers, and get your work done, you could be on our team.

Tommy had an itch that kept him moving all the time. When I think of him, even now, he is always en route to somewhere else. Maybe it was a result of being locked up for so long. He would start out for a stroll and end up four hours later having passed by the workplace or front porch of five or 10 friends that he had stopped to jaw with.

Tommy was what they called on the block a fast talker. He never said anything earth shattering, it was just warm-hearted chatter, and he was so friendly and effortless that he made for great company. I'd round the corner into his domain—the nuts-and-bolts aisle—and just stand and shake my head while he talked some poor customer's ear off. They never seemed to mind. While it's true that we sometimes spent $20 in labor to help somebody find the right 10 cent picture hanger, by the time the customer left his aisle, Tommy had made a new friend, and so had the store.

Right around that time, I was in the market for a store dog. I wanted a Logan Hardware mascot to add personality to the aisles, and escort me to the bank at the beginning and end of every day. For some reason, I had it in my mind that I absolutely, positively had to have a Great Dane.

I have always loved big dogs, HUGE dogs, and Great Danes are, of course, at the top of the list of "huges." To me, they are lithe and elegant—happy beasts—who will cover three urban blocks in just a few graceful strides in order to lick your face as if to say, "Hello, thank God you're home!" It was in this spirit that I had decided one day that we absolutely needed to have a Great Dane as our Logan Hardware mascot. I should start, though, by saying that we already had a dog—an adorable 40-pound mutt whose name, Maluquina, translated from Portuguese meant "Ornery Girl." Malu more than lived up to her moniker.

Malu did not like other dogs. She also hated children. Come to think of it, she also disliked men with hats, squirrels, and wheelchairs. She immediately growled when any creature she did not approve of—of which there were many—entered her field of vision. She was exactly the opposite of what a store dog should be, so we couldn't hire her for the job.

I pored over the Rescue League's website every morning and every night, looking for adoptable Danes. Then finally, one day, there he was. The knock-kneed, doe-eyed, irresistible Great Dane of my dreams. His name was Jay, and he had been living in a trailer park just outside of Baltimore but had been put out because either a) he bit a child or b) his snaggle tooth made him a bad candidate for Best in Show. I called the Rescue League lady, and she told me the kid had only had a scratch on his face when they picked Jay up, so they had pretty much settled on option B being the reason the dog had been abandoned. If a dog that size had bitten the kid, it would have been obvious.

The first thing we had to do was take Malu for a visit to meet Jay. I didn't tell the rescue lady that Malu was most definitely NOT going to like the big brother I was foisting on her, at least not right away. But there was no way around this regrettable meeting. We were not allowed to adopt unless every member of the household passed a "get along" test. Malu had a vote, whether we liked it or not.

We met Jay at a mansion—easily 6,000 square feet in the middle of Baltimore City. Only a place on a palatial scale like that could make a Great Dane seem miniscule by comparison. The Rescue League had picked their headquarters strategically. We were greeted by a man surrounded by FIVE statuesque Danes, all eager to put their paws on our shoulders, lick our faces, and say hello. I was in heaven while Malu tried to burrow her way under the oriental rug in the entryway.

For Jay's tryouts, we made our way to a local, flower-filled park with a fenced-in dog run. Miraculously, Malu kept her composure and did not make a scene or try to dig an escape tunnel to China through the carefully manicured perennial beds.

For an entire hour, we all laughed and interacted and started to bond as a family with Jay. I couldn't believe that Malu was signing off on the deal. The League gentleman approved us on the spot and asked us to return a week later to pick Jay up and take him to his new forever home.

Seven days and six hours later, I was driving home in Marc's BMW convertible with the largest lap dog in the world trying to scrunch himself onto the back ledge of the back seat, which was about a quarter of the size of his body. Nobody had thought to warn me that Jay was afraid of car rides.

And so, life with Jay began not with a bang but a whimper. Marc fell for him, hard. Our plan was that Jay would be a welcoming face in the store and yet, a warning to everyone that a very large beast guarded me as I walked cash to the bank each day. It was so fun walking him to work, although my 12-minute commute on foot turned into a 30-minute stroll because everyone wanted to meet "the horse." Jay was a one-dog parade passing by, and everybody wanted to pet the main attraction.

Sadly, not everybody was as thrilled with the new addition once we were inside the store. Marc and I understood that Jay was a mama's boy and a total mush. Even Malu had bought in. But many of our customers didn't see beyond his gargantuan proportions and were terrified of him. Jay was larger than most everybody who came into the shop.

Customers would spot him in an aisle, stop dead in their tracks, and slowly start to back up. You could almost see the hair on their necks stand up. Before we could explain to them that Jay was a Care Bear in disguise, the customer had turned around and scurried the other way. Honestly, it was hard not to giggle. It had never occurred to us that people might be afraid of Jay, but so many were. In fact, pretty much everyone was spooked except for us and Tommy. Within a few short weeks, we knew there was no way Jay was going to be a store dog.

We tried leaving Jay at home during the day, but this did not go over well at all with the exiled mascot. He felt personally offended and fundamentally terrified of being home alone and he howled nonstop. This really started to annoy our neighbor who got pretty good at howling himself—I would be in the middle of helping a customer when my cell phone would ring.

"Come stop this whining!" Richard would scream before I could even say hello.

There was no doubt about it, our in-the-store turned stay-at-home dog was not a happy camper and we were at our wits end as to what to do about it. Marc and I were so physically and emotionally drained by the time we got home each day that we couldn't give Jay the time and attention he craved. I have always thought that one of my best character traits is my abundance of positive energy, but when that energy hits a wall, well, I am done. I was failing my dream Dane and I felt terrible about it.

Rules for Choosing a Store Dog

○ Don't get swayed by big dogs with big sad eyes. Look for a dog that is happy to see you, and everybody else on first sight.

○ Make sure your dog isn't tall enough to push the panic bar on the fire exit door.

○ Scale your store dog to your store. If you are in a shoebox, get a teacup. If you have wide aisles, you can consider a larger sporting breed. But for heaven's sake, don't try to put a huge dog straight out of an epic Greek myth into your store aisles, or you'll for sure freak out your customers.

○ Pick a dog with an even temper. Enthusiasm is good, but not everybody feels the same way about a dog that can jump up and look you in the eyes while giving you a big smooch.

○ Make sure that you go through a good training program with your store dog. They have to know to listen to you and do what you ask of them. Most importantly, the commands "stay" and "come."

One day, watching Jay throw his paws around Tommy's neck during a visit, I had a jolt of inspiration. Jay and Tommy loved each other. So, I gave Tommy a key to our house and asked him to please start taking Jay along with him on his walkabouts. In no time at all, Tommy was coming by before and after work to gather up his buddy. I'd barely have started my first cup of morning coffee and I'd hear the front door unlock.

Tommy would stroll in, nod his head in my direction and grab the leash. He'd talk to Jay instead of me—as if they knew I needed some quiet time before heading to my retail life. Tommy would talk to the dog as though he could understand every damn word, and watching Jay listen to Tommy, I thought maybe he was right. In some miraculous way, they completed each other.

"Hey Jay," Tommy would say, "Whaddya say we head down Rhode Island Avenue today? Maybe find some bones? Maybe see some of the guys, whaddya think?" Jay would look at Tommy, panting happily, and the two would set about their day's adventure. It was a joy to see them together. Two gentle, misunderstood souls who didn't expect any more from life than long walks and pleasant company. I'm not sure Tommy had gotten much love in life except from his mom, and neither had Jay. Now they were heaping it on each other in Great Dane-size portions.

Those two walked for hours and hours and pretty soon Jay didn't feel like howling any more. Tommy would bring him back home, both visibly content after their day.

The trek often ended with Tommy asking, "When are you going to give me *my* dog, Gina?" I began to think it was a good question.

So, despite the fact that we were really attached to our big guy, after many weeks during which Jay spent more time with Tommy than us, we finally made it official. We handed the leash permanently over to Tommy and his elderly mother who took care of him like a second son until the day Jay died. I can still see Mrs. Carter sitting on the sofa in her pale blue housecoat, sipping the warm beer she favored, stroking Jay's ears, while Tommy dozed in the chair beside her. Jay's eyes would slowly close, until his big ole head fell into Mrs. Carter's well-cushioned lap, and Tommy and Jay would both begin to snore peacefully, dreaming of tomorrow's adventures.

A retail business is built on three things, people, product, and place. For Tommy and Jay, the place had been the missing leg in their stool. They both needed somewhere to shine, where they were valued as an asset, rather than feared as a liability. They both found that place with us. And then they found each other.

Tommy didn't know any of this when he took the job. We didn't either. At the beginning, it was just a little corner hardware store. Little did either of us know that Tommy had found a place where he would work and learn and grow for the next 12 years. And little did Tommy know that he would find his best friend in the form of a 175-pound Great Dane named Jay who had found his own way home from the trailer parks of Maryland to be by Tommy's side.

FOUR

Don't Give Up Five Minutes Before a Miracle

'**ve learned countless** things from Marc over the years, but he has one saying that rises to the top. He likes to say, "You don't have to go out of your way to hire someone—you just have to remove the obstacles to their employment." I had no idea that when we opened the doors to Logan Hardware, my entire world would change based on that mantra. My eyes would be opened, and my leadership abilities would be stretched in ways I could never have imagined, and it all started with Shane.

When Shane first appeared at the front door of Logan Hardware, looking lost and under-nourished, he was only about four weeks into recovery. As he likes to tell it, it was during the time when he couldn't keep a single thought in his head. I could relate. I was so busy back then, I couldn't either. He asked for a job, and I told him I wasn't hiring. He showed up like that for a few days running, and every time I told him no. Then one day, as fate would have it, he showed up just like always, only on that day, the delivery truck had just arrived, and we did need help. I told Shane that he could work the day helping us unload and if he was still happy at the end of the day, he could come back the following week.

So that is how we began, one week at a time when the delivery truck pulled up. Even though he looked like he weighed about a hundred pounds soaking wet, Shane went to work like a man twice his size tanked up on jet fuel. Marc nicknamed him "Lift" because it seemed as though he'd slung 20 times his weight in delivery boxes that first day and then every day thereafter. Lift was a man on a mission.

Shane came back seven days later when the next truck load arrived and helped us again. I paid him in cash, and he told me he'd return the following week, and so it went on like that, week to week, as consistent as clockwork. Soon, he was learning how to put away our product on the shelves. Then he started coming by every day to ask for a permanent role. Every single time I told him no. But I was starting to get used to our daily ritual of rejection and his undimmable enthusiasm, and soon, I found myself really liking Shane. I admired his patience and his persistence, and I loved his infectious smile.

Eventually, Shane started to tell me a little about himself. He had grown up in Charleston, SC, but moved to DC after a long stint in New York City that had ended with 9/11, a bad case of PTSD, and an increasingly self-destructive crystal meth habit. He had come to DC to get clean. He found us because we were right down the street from the Whitman- Walker Clinic where he was a part of a very active recovery program. Shane had watched our store open while en route to his daily meetings, and thought we looked like a safe harbor.

The more I learned about Shane, the more I liked him. Soon, I found myself finding ways to give him more work. I was sticking him into whatever nook or cranny I could find that needed attention. Shane had been an assistant in a hair salon at one point, so I had him start coloring my hair. Marc found a variety of odd jobs for him around the store. He even started cleaning our house. Anything that needed doing, all the loose ends were handed over to Shane so that he could make his ends meet.

I remember Shane cried the day I gave him a key to our place—an innocuous gesture on my part, I thought, but later realized it was a show of confidence he hadn't experienced in a while. No one had trusted him like that in years, and we watched as our belief in turn made him more self-assured and capable. He began to shine from the inside out, and the mutual trust empowered us too. Shane was starting to offer me his first important life lesson—trusting the people who work for you is one of the keystones of a successful business.

Eventually, we got to the point where we could take on Shane full time, and he became one of our most reliable and committed team members.

He was funny, personable and never made customers feel stupid because they asked an obvious question or didn't know how to do something. He helped create our no-judgement atmosphere at Logan Hardware, and customers loved him. Although in a small store everybody works every department, we based Shane in plumbing, an area that left Marc and I both bewildered. Shane would laugh and say "This is ridiculous. How is a gay man supposed to explain to people how male and female parts fit together all day long?"

Quotes Taped to My Desk

I don't have the strongest memory so when an expression jumps out at me, I tape it to my desk. Some have taught me a lesson; some inspire me and all of them will live forever in my brain. Over the years, some of my favorites have been:

- If you're feeling pressure, you're not applying it
- We want a super organization, not super humans
- When faced with a problem ask yourself:
  - What is the challenge?
  - What are my three options?
  - Which one do I choose?
- Eat that frog
- A jobless community is a thankless community
- I was born an original, I won't die a copy
- You're not a clone why shop at one?
- You've gotta earn luck

I've been guilty over the years of saying that folks in recovery make the best employees because they have so much energy. Watching Lift work was clear evidence of that because he just never stopped. He was like the Energizer Bunny—an unstoppable force from the moment he walked in the door until the moment he walked out at the end of each day. I now understand, after employing so many people in recovery, that it is mostly nervous energy that's underneath the constant motion. An addict has to keep moving forward to keep their habit in their rearview mirror. Every day they are outrunning the cravings, so a three-story hardware store with no elevator can come in handy.

Shane stayed with us for 11 months, and then on a random Thursday afternoon in the middle of October, he stormed out like an angry cloud as if we had wronged him. I was standing at the register with one of our regulars when we heard shouting and what sounded like a herd of wild animals on the stairs. We froze as Shane ran past us screaming that we were *terrible employers* and that this was a *horrible place to work*.

"It was self-righteous indignation," he told me much later. "I was angry with the world and wanted everyone around me to feel bad too." It would be several years before we saw him again. Shane had disappeared back into the mist that had delivered him, and the rest, for a little while anyway, was silence.

We carried on, but Shane's departure had left a void. We all felt bad about the way he left, and it really stung that he had felt that he had been mistreated. I wanted Logan Hardware to be a place where everyone felt valued and appreciated. But the truth is, I was too busy trying to figure out how to run a business to think much about anything in detail. I didn't even try to call him to see what we had done so wrong. I felt bad about that too.

I learned some months later from a new employee that despite the way he had left, Shane had been vouching for us across the way at Whitman- Walker ever since. Apparently, after the storm passed, Shane remembered us as he had first recognized us, a safe harbor, where he re-learned how to show up on time and work hard enough to get better. And he did get better and is drug free to this day.

Throughout those first years of Logan Hardware's life, Shane sent people to work for us from his recovery group, and we kept on hiring them. Shane saw in us what we hadn't yet seen in ourselves. We were a place for you to be nurtured but not coddled, a place where you could move forward with some modernized wiring and a fresh coat of paint, emerging on the other side maybe a little better than when you started.

From the day we handed over our housekeys to Shane, just as we had with Tommy, we were leading from a place of trust. This was the beginning of what has grown into a unique culture at our hardware stores. If you trust the people you hire, you have hired the right people.

My Hero, Greg Boyle

Gregory Joseph Boyle, S.J., is the Founder and Director of Homeboy Industries, the world's largest gang-intervention and rehabilitation program, and former pastor of Dolores Mission Church in Los Angeles.[12] Years ago, I was given Father Greg's first book called *Tattoos on the Heart* and it changed my life.

Both this *New York Times* bestseller and his follow up *Barking to the Choir* document how Father Boyle and his team grew to be the largest tattoo removal and job creation program for gang members in the country. Everything he wrote about speaks to me—from the practice of "radical kinship" to the phrase "nothing stops a bullet like a job."[13] The stories and challenges the "homies" overcome could be called miraculous, but I think they're a testament to the resiliency of the human spirit.

Father Boyle believes in the underdog for sure, but his true strength lies in his belief that human beings need a purpose. And if that purpose is a job, not a gang, then good things can happen. I take this lesson to heart and even though on many days it seems impossible to get right, building jobs for people then helping them keep that job is one of my underlying goals in life.

When I find myself needing a kick in the pants to do more, I watch one of Boyle's TED talks or read a passage from one of his books. If rebuilding neighborhoods and piecing lives back together is done with hardware, someone like Father G is the mortar. I'm guessing he'd be pissed if I called him a saint—but I am sure I would not be the first one to do it. Boyle travels around the country giving speeches and he often brings a "homie" or "homegirl" along with him. Many of the men have faces absolutely covered in tattoos or are in some phase of having them removed. You can imagine that most folks are terrified when they run across this crew, whether in the airport, or at a fancy dinner event or in the presence of a priest. Father Boyle knows this. He also knows we can be terrifying to his companions. By exposing them to us, he is exposing us to them.

I don't remember the day Shane eventually rematerialized, but the memory is crystal clear in his mind. He said that he apologized and told me he wanted me to know we were still friends. I told him that I had never thought we weren't.

After that, Shane would come by often to check on us. He wanted to make sure we were keeping our heads above water, and that the people he sent our way were doing a good job of taking care of us, themselves, and the store. By then, he was working for a local restaurant group as Director of Business Development. Our friendship has only strengthened over the years. Shane calls me if he needs advice, and I check in with him when I have a question only he can answer. Sometimes, I just want to hear a friendly voice, to talk to someone who knows where I've been.

In 2021, he presided over the grand opening of his very own restaurant in a very popular neighborhood near the famous Eastern Market in DC, and I am so proud of him.

When I ask Shane now about why he left, he tells me that he had been stressed out about money. He was being evicted again and wasn't taking the time to process what was going on in his life. He felt unable to ask for help. He felt like he was in over his head, so he lashed out at the people who loved him most, the people he knew were safe, who would accept him no matter what.

Today, Shane tells me that his time with us all those years ago helped to teach him a big life lesson—to always remember to take the time to process your feelings, and to trust the people who love you enough to tell them how you are feeling and be willing to ask them for help.

My time with Shane taught me to lead with trust, to never give up on people, because you just never know who might walk through your door and ask for a shot. And as Shane said to me one day while we were unloading a truck, "You never know when you are only five minutes away from a miracle, Gina. How would you feel if you gave up on somebody just five minutes too soon?"

FIVE

There Are No Tears in Hardware

As the boat pulled away from the dock, an older couple sat down next to Marc and me and asked if we were on our honeymoon. Apparently, our newly wedded marital success was shining from our sun kissed faces. Marc still had hair and neither of us had the crow's feet that inch away from our eyes now. After telling us that they had been married for 40 years, the gentleman leaned closer to Marc. "I'm going to give you the key to our marital bliss," he said with a mischievous smile. "We agreed on our honeymoon that she would make all the little decisions and I would make all the big ones. As of today, there have never been any big decisions."

✹✹✹✹✹✹

Young couples can test their marriage in a variety of ways. Certainly, buying a house and surviving international travel like Marc and I had just done are two of them. But not every couple is meant to go into business together; clicking as lovers does not automatically mean a joined c-suite will sing.

So maybe it was fortunate that in the beginning, Marc had never intended to leave his corporate job. He wasn't interested in retail entrepreneurship, and he wanted to make sure he could help pay the rent at Logan Hardware if things didn't take off quite as I hoped. That rent was a staggering $14,000 a month and while Marc wasn't making anywhere near that much money, it gave us both comfort knowing there was at least one stable income.

I did need him to help get the endeavor off the ground though because Ace insisted that I include Marc and his assets on my application. I was irked, but I ignored the red flags. Then, after Richard was canned but before my future as a hardware store owner was officially on solid footing, I was required to bring Marc to a meeting with a group of regional Ace executives.

While Marc had made it clear to Ace in the early days that he wasn't going to have anything to do with the business, he was apparently needed to back me up to make the old boys happy. He sat next to me that day, almost silent the entire time, confident that I knew what I was talking about. Each question lobbed, like "How much do you intend to sell?", "Who is your target audience?", or "How will you market to them?" was directed to Marc but the answers came from me. I had done my homework. I might have been incredibly inexperienced, but I was not uninformed. My passion for this project, this leap to help a community I loved, was not taken lightly. I know now that it might have been 90% exuberance that got me through that meeting, but it was a confident exuberance.

Our bank seemed to have the same attitude toward gender delineation and Marc took time off work to attend those meetings as well. We jumped through weeks of hoops to secure an SBA loan—75% of our loan was guaranteed by the federal government because I didn't have any business ownership experience or a great deal of money in the bank. Marc didn't have those things either, but he is a man, so I guess that counted as important.

Truthfully, I was too excited at the time to be annoyed that I needed my husband to get my plan off the ground. At that point, I was willing to do anything to make sure I could get my store open.

I was having a conversation one day with a young tenant who was at that point renting my first condo. He asked me what would happen if the business failed. "What's the worst thing?"

"I could lose my house, my car, and my dog," I said.

"They'll take YOUR DOG?" he shouted. The horror on his face was almost comical.

Of course, the bank wouldn't want my dog, but they would take the condo the tenant was living in, and I didn't want to alarm him that day. I had signed my life away for at least the foreseeable future—the loan I took out was for 10 years, whether the store was making money or not.

All through those interminable bank meetings, the Ace sit downs, and the myriad mounting pressures we were under, my unflappable husband carried on like it was all completely normal. Where my naïve optimism and hyperactivity kicked into high gear, his calmness presided. Unwilling or unable to upset his new wife, I was on my way to learning that Marc would be extremely supportive of any of "our" ideas. The tedious act of big bank loans was just one of the first big decisions he didn't have to make. He loves to remind me that I once told a friend that I bit off more than *we* can chew.

Months after those initial meetings, the loans were secured, and thousands of products lined our shelves. It didn't matter that I hadn't heard of most of them, much less knew what they were used for. It was time to start making money. It was also time to turn my attention to our young team, so Marc returned to his tech life in the suburbs, and I made my official transition from software to hardware.

❋❋❋❋❋❋

It was, at this point, that our inaugural team started to write the history of our start up, giving it their all right beside me. We were a bit of a ragtag crew who grew to be a family.

Jen, the store's first real cashier, rolled in every day, steady as sunshine.

She lived in the big apartment building just across the alley, right behind the store, and had stopped by to ask for a job one day when we were setting up. I told her we weren't hiring. For someone who has a really hard time saying no, my early days were dotted with turning down requests from folks who would serendipitously become integral parts of our story.

Less than a week later, opening day came around, and I completely panicked. This was my first time at bat. Not only had I never had to staff a retail business before, I also hadn't been set up for success. The Ace team, continuing to doubt my viability, had advised me to hire only four employees.

Also, there was the issue of our wildly odd configuration. Logan Hardware was 100 feet deep, 20 feet wide, three levels, no elevator, no loading dock, no parking. NO, NO, NO. Maybe Ace was right to think I was nuts? But with 5,000 square feet and some *minor* logistical challenges, I should have known that a team of four would never be enough.

Next, I learned how to make keys and paint the day we opened our doors. These two product categories were to become the backbone of our revenue and I launched a business with almost no knowledge of them. These days I am happy to consult about projects that include words like sheen or coverability, but back then all I could see were rows and rows of paint cans taunting me from a few central aisles. A little training in advance would have really come in handy.

Hardware Bloopers (Tips for the DIYer)

- Move your thumb when you swing the hammer
- Don't drink beer until AFTER you've painted the walls
- Turn off the water supply before pulling a faucet out of the wall
- Always buy more than one mousetrap
- Measure twice, cut once
- There is no such thing as a male-to-male electrical plug

So, with the cash tills freshly filled with change and the ink barely dry on our sign, I realized at the very last moment that I was embarrassingly shorthanded. At this point, though, it seemed too late to do anything about it.

Fate smiled at me that day, because as I bent down to sweep up a pile of dust into the dustpan, a tiny scrap of paper with Jen's number on it peeked out from the trash. I called her immediately and she started working that very day. Reliable, personable and a little bit of a gambler, Jen helped make the long days more enjoyable. On Saturdays, she and I would bet on how soon we could sell $500's worth of stock in one hour. Then $3000's worth for the day, then $5,000. Those days were like a 10-hour workout and math gymnastics at the same time.

At some point, we hired Eric, a wonderfully cheesy and incredibly sweet young man from Indiana who had grown up on a farm. He liked to say *yeppers* a lot and we teased him incessantly about it. He was a young Republican living in a city where 98% of the populace is Democrat and I always admired his courage. He eventually moved on to several successful government jobs and ultimately to the suburbs to start his family. For years after he left, he would invite Marc and me to lunch during the holidays to thank us again for helping him get his city legs when he first moved to Washington. His midwestern graciousness was a reminder that you can never say thank you enough and that any job can propel you into your future.

Eddie was 14 when he came to the store for his interview. He was growing up in public housing down the street and lived with his mother, who seemed so young to be raising a teenager. He was also painfully shy. The community organizer who brought him to the store did all the talking as Eddie looked down at his feet. I would ask a question, look at Eddie for the answer, and the words would come from the man sitting next to him. The conversation triangle should have made me worry about future customer service efforts, and I wasn't even sure I was legally allowed to offer a 14-year-old a job, but I did, and Eddie stayed for 11 years while we watched him grow into a confident young man.

I could tell stories about dozens of great folks who were integral that first year, but the most important employee development by far brings the story full circle.

Marc came home from his day job three months after I had opened Logan Hardware and proclaimed that he was "working too hard doing two jobs"—his own and helping me at the store. "If you'll have me, I'd like to join the team for real," he said.

"Besides," Marc continued, "you're having too much fun without me." He put his arm around me, gave me a kiss and laughed, and just like that, he committed to the store full time. I am sure I did cartwheels—I certainly should have. It was truly great news.

I'm not sure Marc realized how much his involvement meant to me early on and I don't know if I've thanked him as much as I should have. He was there 500%, right from the very beginning. He was there when the bank needed more and more collateral. He was there to help unload the first Ace truck that arrived in a snowstorm with 40,000 pounds of shelving, and he was there to coin one of our first and favorite mantras: *There are no tears in hardware.* There is no whining on Marc Friedman's watch, and if

I get myself (or him or us or them) into a mess, I am under no circumstances going to cry my way out of it!

Marc's steadfast support and belief in me was enough to get me out of bed every day. From that day forward we were a team, a legit mom and pop hardware store. If silos are built into a marriage—a delineation of chores and responsibilities, it typically works. You know, he takes out the trash and she makes the grocery list kind of stuff. But we had all new lessons to learn when business co-ownership entered the mix.

If we had set out to marry and work with our mirror opposite, we couldn't have done a better job of it. We were as different as hammer and nail, but where some traits diverged, others complemented each another in ways that have made us fantastic business partners.

✺ ✷ ✹ ✸ ✺ ✷

For starters, we are both very trusting people, and this trust was the glue that helped our company culture develop and solidify. When Shane ran out, yelling that we were terrible employers, it didn't launch us into planning an employment strategy that avoided hiring people in recovery. In fact, we did the opposite almost without knowing it.

We deal with theft on a daily basis, for example, but our strong belief that people are inherently good enables us to let it go so we can get on with our jobs. Equally, expansion doesn't happen when one micromanages from a place of distrust, and we became good at growing both jobs and locations.

I am not good at sweating the small stuff, but Marc is. So, I look for the bigger picture and growth and he thankfully pulls the pieces together. When I was ready to look for new communities to grow in, Marc and the team took the reins to make it happen. He also eventually took over all the banking meetings—funny, they never needed me to attend.

Life's greatest pairs often have someone in front who is carried by someone behind the scenes. And I will argue all day long that it's that person, the one who doesn't always command the spotlight, who does the heavy lifting.

Consider a successful waitress who is backed up by runners and busboys. She smiles, takes an order, and collects the big tip. I know the job is much more nuanced than that, but the whole show works because of the backup singers. They function as a team, and they win as one. In working relationships that include life as well as business partners, it might be smart to emulate a successful wait staff.

Getting Publicity

It was amusing to me in those early days how enamored the press was with the idea of a woman-owned hardware store, so we gave them what they wanted. I was comfortable with a microphone in my face, Marc preferred to leave the interviews up to me. We were and are both still slightly mortified by the American Gothic reproduction of us that the *Washington Post* published in 2006 but we were happy with seeing the store name in the press as often as possible.[14]

It's not hard to imagine that we are often asked what it's like to work with our spouse and that our answers can vary widely. Depending on the day, you'll get an eyeroll or a shoulder shrug as part of the answer. "It's no big deal" may be the words that accompany the gesture. But to be clear, if I had married someone more like myself, we would have unraveled early on.

One of our early challenges was settled by a peer in the industry who chastised us for separating our leaders into "mine" and "his." Like the marriage silos with individual to-do lists, we made the mistake of dividing our team based on our own skill sets and interests, which ended up causing constant unalignment. Marc is better at numbers, so he worked more closely with the Inventory Manager and our Buyer. I push the people angle so I spent more time with our HR and Marketing Managers. It seems like a logical division of labor, but when we started to pit them against each other, we had to reassess.

"You are all on the same team," our friend said. "Stop trying to keep them apart." After that we all started meeting as one team, and more consistently, so we could all provide input to each other. Even if we hear things differently, at least we start out in the same room.

Not long after that, we hired a business coach to work with us—she helped us craft our core values and solidify a bunch of procedures, but most importantly she had us all take a personality assessment, which helped us understand our differences and taught us how to communicate better with one another. With our personality traits laid bare, Marc stood up and announced to the room hilariously that he "now understands every fight he's ever had with his wife." In the end, it was just the lesson we all needed, but it didn't completely stop future hiccups.

✵✵✵✵✵✵

Our style differences caught up to us one fateful day 15 years after the business began. That day, Ann Marie (our Director of Human Resources), Marc, and I sat around our conference table strategizing about fall staffing needs and some of our operational challenges. Marc, who sometimes thinks he's been clear ("clear as mud," my dad says) was sure he was accurately explaining that we were overspending on salaries and that our revenue wasn't keeping up. He also thought that we were just blatantly ignoring him. He later mused:

"I don't know what they were thinking! I am sure they heard exactly what I said, and Gina's reaction was to pretend to ignore it. Ann Marie, to her credit, heard and understood it perfectly and was the one who ultimately made the changes for us. I am sure to this day that it wasn't a communication issue. Maybe the question was one of urgency or severity, but not communication."

If I noticed the steam coming out of his ears, I didn't acknowledge it until he came absolutely unhinged. He stood up, yelled that we were going to go out of business and that obviously, "You don't give a shit." Then he stormed out. Ann Marie and I were stunned. I had never seen him so angry. He never raises his voice and, to be honest, he hadn't gotten his point across, so we didn't know what he was angry about. I gave him a few minutes to cool off, remaining in my chair to chat with Ann Marie until

I jogged off down the hall to find him. His office was dark, his chair empty. My normally composed husband was so mad that he had actually gone home. The gravity of the situation sunk in at that point.

When we were together later that day, he related that in his head he had been crystal clear—concise, articulate, and raving mad. It was a good reminder of something I had learned during my freshmen orientation at Wittenberg—*your roommate cannot read your mind.*

We eventually worked through the severe financial instability our staffing levels had created and launched methods for tracking productivity that we use to this day. But we had to acknowledge that no matter how long we have been married or working together, our silos need to merge and collaborate and most importantly, we need to hear what each other is saying.

These days, we acknowledge that we get on each other's nerves at least once a day but would still rather spend our time together than with anyone else. Honestly, the fact that he won't put the dishes in the dishwasher is probably more annoying than any of Marc's business traits. But I'll take that any day.

🌼🌼🌼🌼🌼🌼

That first year, the days were long and breaks were few, but I don't remember anything but high spirits and hard work. We ran up and down those steps incessantly, trying to learn what things were used for so we could help every customer who walked through our door. We introduced words into our vocabulary that became so common that for years they were on our work vests—thingamabobs, whatchamacallits, and thingamajigs.

Thanksgiving was soon approaching, and I found myself thinking about how thankful I was for every member of our team. It was our first legitimate day off in months and we knew exactly who we wanted to spend it with. We decided to host the entire cast of characters for dinner at our place and began a tradition of closing for some big holidays so our team could enjoy time with their families, whether blood related or not.

Most of our families lived far away, and we wouldn't be able to get to them so why not put on a big ol' mess of a meal at our place, and invite the Thanksgiving orphans over for dinner?

Dishes from the Recovery Hardware Global Table

- Lasagna
- Chitterlings
- Quesadillas
- Sweet Potato Pie
- Gramma Annabelle's loaf stuffing

We asked everyone to bring a dish that reminded them of Thanksgiving with their own families, and we supplied the bird. All I can say about the feast that resulted is *Wow!* An amazing array of unpredictable and delicious food wound up on our table. It was glorious, as visually delicious as it was tasty.

I grew up around a traditional Midwestern table—the staples were turkey, stuffing, mashed potatoes, gravy, corn, and biscuits. You know, all the beige food. But that year we had bright, vibrant dishes like lasagna, quesadillas, chitlins, green chili, and sweet potato pie. It was a multicultural, multicolored and delicious reflection of everyone around the table. We were building a team that looked like the world—like the beautiful city where we lived.

Fat and happy after the last person left, Marc asked if we could repeat the event a week later *just for the hell of it*. I wasn't sure about that one, but it has been a favorite memory since the minute our last guest arrived. Kathleen, Drew, Jen, Tommy, William, Rachel, Scott, Wasson, Laura, Lisa, James: the list, we realized, had become a long one.

The lines between boss and employee disappeared that day. We had become a family. There have been times when my heart has been broken because of that bond—a special teammate betrays us or leaves abruptly—but closeness is always worth the pain. The house felt so warm that day, full of jokes and stories. It was a holiday to remember, and the first of many with our hardware family which grows bigger and better every year. Thankfully, we have become a team that, just like our Thanksgiving table and our incredible neighborhoods, feels like home.

Logan Circle Grows Up

Between 2000 and 2015, Washington, DC added 100,000 residents and the city just kept getting better.[15] With about 600,000 residents in 2003 and well over a million who commuted in and out every day, the measly four or five hardware stores in the city weren't cutting it. One of the neighborhoods that had experienced the biggest population growth was our Logan Circle, and we got to see just about everybody who moved in at some point or another shopping our aisles. Whether Black, White, brown, gay, straight, a single mom or a dad with three kids, you were going to need something from a hardware store, and that meant you were going to meet us.

After we opened, a whole host of other businesses started popping up and the neighborhood really came alive. Developers were having a field day turning old buildings and vacant lots into condominiums and other masterpieces. Stores like Home Rule, Vastu, Go Mama Go and Pulp all vied for attention with new restaurants like Logan Tavern, Rice, and the urban transplant, Stoney's. These places were always packed—patronized by a community that was thrilled to have them. The Main Street feel that had been lost on that terrible day in 1968 was starting to make a comeback.

Thinking of the neighborhood back then, I always envision Mayberry—folks going about their day, headed out on errands and talking to store owners whose first names and histories they all knew. I always made it a point to stop by Pulp, a paper and gift store owned by Ron Henderson, a man whom I loved from the minute I met him. A big bear of a man, Ron opened his first boutique in an old 2nd floor hair salon because his build-out was talking too long and damnit, he had products to sell!

Ron was the type of person who made a room glow just by walking in—being near him would warm you up and make you smile. I learned a lot from the welcoming way he did business. He opened his second location in Provincetown, married the man of his dreams, and then succumbed to cancer and died in 2009. We were all devastated. Pulp stayed open for a few years after that, but truth be told, it was never profitable. Ron and his pal Beverly were the secret sauce, sourcing slightly naughty greeting cards and having just the perfect gift when we needed one. The store motto was "Come feel the love" and if they were around, you really, really did.

SIX

If You're Feeling the Pressure, Push Back

Paolo Coehlo once wrote, "When you want something, all the universe conspires to help you achieve it."[16] Well, one day in 2004, the universe conspired to give me exactly what I wanted, in the form of a car door and some very hard pavement. I was headed to work—it was only a seven-minute bike ride, but I was late—and I hate being late. Marc was riding behind me and saw the whole thing unfold, without enough time to warn me. I turned the wrong way onto a one-way street and hurled myself knee first into the door of an oncoming car. I bounced forward and immediately ricocheted back, landing on the hard ground, flat on my back.

The second I hit the pavement, I burst into tears—big sobs racked my body as neighbors rushed outside to help, assuming that I was broken into bits. Remarkably, I was fine—my knees were scraped and would definitely turn black and blue by morning, but the blood was blottable with only one sorry tissue. Oh, and my ass hurt really bad where I had landed on it. That was it. Kind of pathetic really, given the scale of my outburst. That's because the sobbing wasn't out of pain or injury. It was due to a culmination of bottled-up stress that just needed a reason to release. That car door had just given me my excuse.

Everyone who knows me will confirm that I am incapable of micro-managing anything, and yet, for months, I had been attempting to manage every single detail involved with the operation of Logan Hardware. From hiring, to training, to customer service—I had been trying to master it all so that I could then train others. This, as the concrete had just taught me, was not a good management model. I needed some people around who were good at things I wasn't good at. And that was when the universe delivered Mark Wasson to our front door.

When he found us, Wasson was six months into treatment for a whole host of addictions including alcohol, crystal meth, and gambling. He was, I will admit, a somewhat nontraditional guardian angel. Wasson was successfully and (miraculously) living with HIV and had heard from Shane, my one-man PR machine, that we would probably give him a job.

Wasson grew up near Richmond, VA and after losing a dear friend to suicide in 1994, he moved to DC with his partner to start a new life. Prior to finding us, Wasson had been working in a juvenile correctional facility in Richmond, which he said had been emotionally challenging. His first job in DC was with a residential youth services program where he would hone his patience and nurture his love of teaching—talents I would be lucky enough to see him pick back up later in his life.

I hired Wasson on the spot, and he went to work in the plumbing department. No one wanted to work in the plumbing department. There were easily 5,000 separate pieces of merchandise, three quarters of which you'd never heard of and would never want to. It hardly seemed fair of us to assign anyone to that department, much less someone early in their recovery who was working on redeveloping self-esteem and better coping strategies. But Wasson was tough. He hadn't come this far without some serious mental fortitude. And he seemed to enjoy the challenge.

He was fairly patient with customers and was great at explaining how to use the pieces and parts he recommended. It was easy to see that he enjoyed imparting his knowledge of widgets and thingamajigs to willing listeners. He was also good at researching an answer if he didn't know something. This is a very useful skill to have in the hardware business and doesn't come naturally to everyone. It's hard to find people who are willing to admit when they don't know something, and reach out to educate themselves, and their customers.

Wasson's part of the store was not very attractive, and it always seemed a little damp. The plumbing aisles were accessed by walking up a flight of creaky wooden stairs from the first floor, making a left past the doorknobs and weather-stripping and then up three more wooden stairs to the very back of the store. Customers were exhausted by the time they arrived. Many complained the plumbers most of all. Those with a sense of humor thanked us for saving them a trip to the gym.

The path to the plumbing department had wooden floors that reminded me of a "real" old-timey hardware store. They were beautifully scuffed and semi-worn from a century of use. Once you ascended those last three steps, there were only three aisles, which had very little natural light. Rainy days brought rivers of funk, because the one existing window always leaked. No manner of caulking and re-caulking seemed to fix what a 100-year-old building didn't want sealed.

Despite all of this, Wasson proudly kept his department spotless. In his aisles, every price tag was in place, every product dusted, a testament to his pride of place. Our office was back there—a now-defunct commercial elevator shaft that once carried cars from the first floor to the second. Yep, this oddly shaped row house that we now called a hardware store was a car dealership for a time in the 50s and the elevator was big enough to transport a car from the basement to the showroom floor upstairs.

When the elevator died, it was, thank God, on the bottom floor. Rather than pay the thousands of dollars it would take to remove it, we built our loading dock on the ground level, and then an office in the open space on the second floor. It was a forgotten space, unadorned, overlooked, just a place holder for a desk and chair. The price per square foot for retail space is expensive and we learned early on that there were no dimes to waste to make pretty spaces in which to do paperwork.

The aisles in the plumbing department were roughly 50 feet long and what little wall space you could see was made of the original brick. We liked to say that what it lacked in insulation, it made up for in character. Most of the condos being built in the neighborhood in those days had exposed brick walls and visible heating ducts on purpose. This made Logan Hardware seem like one of the trendy, high-priced minimalist spaces of the moment. Only ours was the real deal!

True to Wasson's nature, he learned and loved that he could help people all day long. In that grimy, sunless place, the self-esteem that had gone down the toilet started to re-emerge. I could tell it delighted him, like he had never expected to feel good about himself again.

Despite his professionalism, Wasson's customer service skills did occasionally need some tweaking. While helping a somewhat distraught young woman pick out a mouse trap one day, he handed her a package containing four traps. When she told him she only needed one trap he informed her matter-of-factly that, "You do know there is never just one mouse, right?" at which point the customer burst into tears. He handed her a tissue and sent her on her way to the cash register, four traps in hand.

Wasson might sound like the perfect teammate, but he had one big area of weakness that really threatened to get in his way (and mine, as it turned out). Wasson did not trust technology. Automation in retail—at least in small retail—has taken on a whole new meaning in the last five or 10 years, but this was 2004, and our industry was so outdated that any technology was a leap out of the dark ages. We had cash registers and that was about it.

We stored change in a tiny rotary safe visible on a shelf under where the cashiers stood. We didn't count our inventory, and my husband Marc would put deposits in a backpack and walk them to the bank no matter how many thousands of dollars were in the till on any given day. It would be years before we hired armored cars and it took two things to ultimately make that happen—the increasing difficulty in finding rolls of quarters and an armed robbery. We were almost religiously old school.

The most tedious task for us was the weekly order, which took precious time away from helping customers. We employed a sophisticated method, an old wooden clipboard—scored at a thrift store to save us the $1.50 that a new one's one would cost—and a pencil. Wasson would walk the aisles, look for peg hooks that seemed light on inventory or were empty, and he would make a note on his spreadsheet. He did this for 15,000 items every single week.

It was damn near a full-time job to do the reordering manually like this, and there was no way I could ever find somebody else who could do it. It made employing Wasson mandatory. He had created job security for life because it would take months to train somebody to do what he was doing, the way he was doing it. How could I ever replace him, or the method?

My tango with the car door had finally convinced me that I needed to offload some of the hands-on work I had been doing. If I was going to grow and scale the business, I had to stop trying to wear every hat in the store. I was going to have to delegate and automate, and that meant that so was Wasson. Fortunately, the corporate Ace inventory team introduced an automated version of this inventory tedium five months into Wasson's tenure and I thought our problem was solved.

"Imagine the beauty and simplicity of ordering thousands of items with the push of a button," I told him, smiling, my eyes wide and inviting, beckoning him to enter this miraculous new world of time-saving technology. I thought Wasson was going to be delighted, but instead he was just pissed. There was absolutely no way to explain to him how a computer could do a better job than he could by walking the aisles and looking at the products with his own two eyes.

Wasson pushed back so hard and so often that eventually I saw that something, or rather someone, had to give. And it wasn't going to be me. Wasson had to move forward, but he was refusing to budge.

Once a blessing of efficiency, Wasson was now holding me back. But I wasn't ready to give up on him. Not quite yet. I tried a new approach. I started to think of Wasson as one of those reluctant football players back in college who just needed a little patience and guidance to get him to fulfill his service requirements. I pulled my Wittenberg lessons forward and went to work trying to acquaint Wasson with the idea of change.

"Just give it a try!" I would say to him, uselessly. "What do you have to lose?" It didn't take long to realize that this line of questioning wasn't getting us anywhere either. I needed Wasson to see the bigger picture. His vision of what we could become was way too narrow for the kind of progress I envisioned. Where was I going wrong that I couldn't get this vital employee to see what I saw? Maybe this tangle had as much to do with my leadership skills as it did with Wasson's fear of progress.

One day, I asked Wasson to describe our management style and he said, "Help the customer get what they need and preferably get them to pay for it before they leave." It would seem that we were a little more wishy-washy than the detail-oriented Wasson would have liked, and this was contributing to his overall sense of anxiety. My laid-back attitude reflected my real desire to first make people love us, then get them to pay us, and those priorities were in the wrong order. It wasn't a sustainable, professional process and Wasson knew that.

Wasson craved structure, rules and guidelines. I know now that these are principles that can also aid people in recovery and help them feel safe enough to make some small adjustments. I, on the other hand, wanted a free-flowing day where everyone just got things done in their own way, in their own time. These were two very different visions: I was water, Wasson was oil, yet I needed him in the mix. Wasson argued his case by explaining that when you get a grip on something, anything, especially in the early throes of recovery, it's hard to let go for fear of the world falling apart. It's like dropping the life raft before you jump off the side of a boat. You're not sure if you'll find it again once you hit the water. I was a young leader and Wasson was teaching me that if I wanted my employees to feel comfortable taking a leap of faith with me, then I had to help build a better raft. One that they could see clearly and feel safe in when the seas got choppy.

Wasson had found a safe harbor with us in his archaic hardware niche that he could control by hand. But we did not have the luxury of sitting back and keeping him comfortable while the business was struggling to grow. While I understood Wasson's hesitation and misgivings, I am not a fan of bowing to resistance. I can acknowledge the pain a change might be causing someone, but I will nevertheless push forward and move through it, and they will either come with me, or they won't. End of story.

In the end, I told Wasson that if he wanted to work for us, he had to get on board.

"This bus is moving, and I want you on the ride with us," I said. "But if you're not up for the journey, then get off the bus."

"Okay," he said reluctantly. "I'll take the training for the new inventory system." In that moment, you could have pushed me over with a feather. I couldn't believe it. I was overjoyed. I had drawn a boundary, and it worked. Wasson studied the training. I left him alone, waiting to see what would happen, and miraculously, about a week or so later, Wasson announced:

"Okay, I'll run the new program simultaneously with my old system."

I said, "Okay." I figured baby steps were better than no steps, and several weeks later, Wasson was comfortable switching over to the new automated system entirely.

I watched his learning curve evolve and followed along with Wasson every step of the way. There was only one catastrophic setback early in the process that threatened to shut the whole thing down. It's funny in hindsight but it just about sent Wasson over the edge. He was called at home one night by our buyer, who was equally green in her role. She had accidentally found and pushed a *delete all* button that had erased the entire order.

This button no longer exists in the system, thank goodness, but Wasson had one final chance to say, "And that is why it's better to do this by hand!" I rolled my eyes, and we laughed. We both knew who had won that argument.

Wasson continued to grow with us—he moved into an Assistant Manager role and then he was put in charge of IT. Yep! The guy who hated technological advancement was put in charge of our software and hardware, at least for a little while.

Wasson's inventory tips:

○ If you see something, say something. Preferably soon after you saw it, so you don't forget it.

○ Even if you can't find it, it is most likely there (somewhere). Keep looking.

○ Count smart and do the math, it makes for fewer footsteps.

○ If you are ordering three or more, or it costs $10 or more, get a second set of eyes on the situation.

○ When in doubt, zero it out.

○ Clipboards are more than just a way to write on a hard surface while in motion.

These days, Wasson manages inventory for our entire chain. Millions of dollars' worth of products are taken care of under his watchful eye—a role he and his computer have excelled at now for 12 years. His old trusty clipboard still hangs on the little green hook right behind his desk, a reminder of how far he has come since that first day. We moved forward together into a future where we didn't have to learn quite as many lessons the hard way, and without bouncing off the concrete.

SEVEN

Even Secret Gardens Need Sunlight

t's nearly impossible to find an unhappy customer in the plant department at Logan Hardware. This leafy oasis grows right under our third-floor office space and I've been known to daydream about stalks of flowers bursting up through the floor on their way to meet the sun.

Most of our guests wandering around this department are looking for something colorful to brighten their day or a living token to give as a gift and I am more than willing to consult on the perfect flowerpot or a pretty sansevieria whenever anybody asks. It doesn't matter if they have never grown anything in their lives—the possibilities are just too big and beautiful to ignore.

"I work in an office with no windows, what can I grow?" might be one of my favorite questions. The most confident of the bunch try repeatedly to make a sunless go of it. It might shock you to learn that I lead them to a display of artificial plants because nothing can grow without at least a little time in the sun. The effort that goes into stocking, pricing, watering, and loving the hundreds of plants that find their way onto our shelves is unbelievable and finding knowledgeable garden department employees is not easy. They must understand both plants and people—a rare combination that only the brightest and most agile are able to master.

One day in 2020 I snuck away to my favorite little spot among the plants as I often do, to take a break from the daily grind. I found myself wandering the aisles, pruning some houseplants and listening to the chatter of my teammates working the afternoon shift. Carl is the lead associate in the garden department, and you can find him there most days giving customers expert advice and chatting everyone up like they are all old friends.

"Now this is the *perfect* plant for your basement apartment. It seems to thrive in low light," he'd say confidently, and he'd start leading the guest to the appropriate soil and plant food. Or he'd offer that "All the grandmothers I know absolutely love Gerbera daisies in their garden," as if he knew all the grandmothers in town, let alone what their favorite flower was.

Words of Wisdom from the Saints of our Garden Departments

- ⚙ Yes, it's true that cacti need much less water (but they STILL need SOME water)
- ⚙ When you go on vacation, don't forget to leave water within reach of your favorite plants
- ⚙ Give them names

- Plants can sense emotions, be kind to them
- Feed the soil, not the plant
- Feel free to talk to your plants as you care for them, but should they happen to respond...listen carefully

Everything Carl said sounded genuine and professional—probably because it was. One would think he had been in the gardening business his whole life. But that couldn't be further from the truth. Carl grew up in St. Louis and had recently turned 54. He had actually only been working with us for four years but had cultivated a following that was envied by our younger associates.

That day, I overheard him, an aisle or so away from where I was standing, telling one of those teammates that he had just celebrated six years clean and that he hadn't expected anyone to come to his sobriety anniversary party because of the pandemic.

Celebrating any milestone with our team members is important but this type of celebration has special meaning and gets double credit in my book. When I hear my teammates discuss their sober-versaries, it's like they are celebrating the most special holiday on earth. If our actual birth gives our parents a reason to celebrate, this self-given rebirth belongs to them alone. It is a day that is hard-won and overwhelmingly deserved. My skin tingled hearing his words. Six years clean is a huge accomplishment, so my curiosity got the best of me and I came out from where I was lurking in the shadows to join the conversation.

"How long did you use drugs?" I asked, knowing he wouldn't mind if there were customers within earshot. He was proud of his accomplishment and didn't care who knew about it.

"Gina, I was an addict and homeless for 14 years," he said in his usual chipper tone. I had a hard time keeping my composure. The man I had lunched with and learned from for four years had lived behind a dumpster or on a park bench for 14 years and I had had no idea. While I traveled the world and built a business and snuggled in my warm bed, Carl had struggled to survive.

"I would hang out in the food court at Union Station and when people left food on their trays I would slide in and finish it like it had been mine all along," he explained to me, and then added with a wistful smile, "I knew people knew it wasn't mine. Gina, if my higher power took me tomorrow, I would be okay with that because the beauty of my last six years has been that good."

I was so touched by his words, and at my new understanding of my plant expert's story. Carl's secrets, like our hidden garden department, need to find their light, and bloom for the world. When we hear from people like Carl we get a bigger sense of real life, we are forced into moments of empathy and greater understanding. There is only one way to grow in this life and that's to understand and empathize with the experiences of others.

I once heard a successful entrepreneur say, "I didn't have the advantage of going to prison," while he was talking to formerly incarcerated entrepreneur, Marcus Bullock about his company Flikshop. Marcus was telling the audience about the inspiring and circuitous route he had taken from maximum security to start-up.

I am sure the speaker was not trying to romanticize a prison sentence or life in a cell, but a message immediately popped up in the chat box with an attendee exclaiming, "Ain't no advantage going to prison."

What he was trying to do, I think, was disassociate physically *being* in a prison cell with having a moment of empathy that allowed him to understand the plight of those in prison. Perhaps he could find kinship where shared experiences did not exist.

Empathy is the ability to understand and share the feelings of another. And not just recognize—but truly comprehend what an action, event or words can do and mean to a person.

I wish that I had documented the powerful moments of empathy I've experienced throughout the years—the ones that have changed how I think, feel or perceive the world. When did I first truly empathize with someone of the Jewish faith, or with an African American, or a single mother or a person with a disability? Who have I not yet had that moment of empathy for? What made something click in my head and heart that then grew there—with more and more clarity each day until it just became *a thing*, something I could not un-feel? Do you remember moments like this in your own life?

Some moments of empathy hit you in the gut, like the overwhelming solidarity I felt when the #MeToo movement started. Others might sink in a bit more gradually but eventually empathy changes the way you think about an entire population. I grew up in a small, very homogenous town. There were no "others" we had to learn to understand. We were mostly Catholic, mostly middle class, and we were all white.

My path from that town to the much larger city of Washington, DC has been full of lessons in empathy that I suspect aren't over yet. People often ask me who or what inspires me. Inspiration can come from anyone or anywhere if you're open to it—books, movies, and of course, people. My thoughts go immediately to my teammates like Carl who teach me something new every day, and especially those in recovery. If you've read this far, surely you've gotten a taste of their perseverance and grace.

I challenge you to cut sugar out of your diet, go to bed earlier or put your phone away at 7 p.m. every evening. Attempt to give up something that you do or rely on every single day. Try doing this for a day, then a week, then a month, then FOREVER.

These are legal, normal, everyday habits that most human beings cannot seem to kick, even though we are told repeatedly that forming positive habits are good for us. My teammates have made lasting habits of kicking some of the most addictive substances known to man. How could I not be inspired by that?

Dry January

When I stopped drinking alcohol completely one "Dry January," I had no idea how long my teetotalling would last, or that my experiment would become a lifestyle. I discovered that for me, the act of not consuming alcohol was the easy part. It was changing how others thought about it that knocked me flat. I had one friend tell me that I "wasn't as fun anymore" when I saw her, and it hurt my feelings every time. While I seethed on the outside, my inside voice was whimpering. What if she was right? How have all my teammates adapted to life without drugs or alcohol if their entire support group was comprised of people who only wanted to hang out with them when they were fucked up?

So many of my teammates over the years have made a lasting impact on my business acumen and my life. In early 2017, I was walking through the kitchen and heard this old guy talking about his 10th half marathon. At 64 years old, he had just run it THAT weekend. You should be able to tell by that sentence that I am just as guilty of bias as anyone but there is no way by looking at Mike that anyone would think he was an avid runner. Soft spoken with a gravelly voice, Mike's speed is a lot more turtle than hare and I got the impression that this is how he had made it through some long, tough years in his life. The fascinating thing about Mike, however, was that he had only become a runner about four years ago because of a non-profit program called "Back on My Feet," which helps homeless people get their life back, one step at a time.

Since getting involved with Back on My Feet, Mike not only has gainful employment and a place to live, but he has run hundreds of miles and dozens of races. On any given day you can ask him about his last race, his next race and the race after that. His experience led him to work to get others who are living on the street involved as well and you can sense the frustration in his voice when he can't get other homeless men to listen to him.

Unfortunately, in 2020, Mike suffered a stroke, which forced him to hang up his running shoes. One day, while hoping to get an update on his condition, a teammate named Lonte approached me on the salesfloor.

After an initial greeting, Lonte launched into a soliloquy that began with: "You know I've known Mike for 19 years, right? We were in prison together. I used to tell him that he should stop using drugs because I had two uncles who were addicts and they got clean. Then Mike got out of prison before me and when I finally did, I found out he had stopped using drugs too. I was so glad—it was like he had listened to some of the things I said."

I stood there, stunned. Nothing came out of my mouth except "hmm, that's real great" (clearly not knowing exactly what to add to this conversation). In the span of 2.5 seconds, I had learned that Lonte had been in prison and that Mike was a recovering addict. No secrets from the boss on my watch. What could I do but nod and smile—bearing witness to the power of a village.

When I'm contemplating how we can change our business or infuse a new "something," I channel Mike. Indeed, one of my frustrations as a leader is when I'm unable to get someone to just try something new—to push past the fear and think "what if?" and go for it. Maybe, just maybe, they will finish the race. With the diversity that surrounds me daily in Washington, D.C., I can say that empathy, and my desire to just understand people better—has helped create all kinds of "moments" for me. I didn't need to write these moments down to remember them. They've permeated my psyche and shaped how I continue to live. And I know they've made my business stronger.

Why does this matter? I often think about our customers interacting with someone on my team who may, or let's face it, probably does have a very different background or life experience to many of them. Like the customer wandering through the plant department and happening upon Carl. I wonder sometimes, what would people think if they knew the truth about the person helping them? Would they sympathize? Empathize? Be disgusted or afraid? Or, like me, would they think "Wow! what an experience this person has lived and overcome."

EIGHT

Hardware Stores Are Not One Size Fits All

One morning while I was working at the register, a man named Paul London walked into the store with a mutual friend who knew we had been talking about expanding. After just a few minutes of chitchat, Paul offered us a spot in a building he owned just two miles away in a neighborhood called Glover Park.

We didn't have to think about it for long. We jumped at the chance to tour the space, fell in love with it at first sight and started hatching plans to move in almost immediately. After all, what reason did we have to hesitate? We knew what we were doing. Logan Hardware was thriving. What could go wrong? Famous last words!

Glover Park was an elegant neighborhood, very different in tone and feel from Logan Circle and on the surface, seemed like a much easier nut to crack. The neighborhood was bordered by Rock Creek Park on the western edge, and the National Cathedral to the north. The Naval Observatory where the Vice President lives was practically in our backyard. It was a real step up from Logan Circle. The building itself was one level, a big rectangle with a fantastic basement for storage which also made everything easier than it was at Logan. We boldly signed on for two and a half times our Logan rent.

I was determined not to hand the Ace corporate team a reason to freak out and say no to me this time around. I did things in the proper order and asked them for approval *before* signing the lease. On the surface, the neighborhood was a much more suitable place to open a business. There wasn't a boarded-up house or vacant lot in sight, and it was adjacent to the well-heeled Georgetown shopping district and Georgetown University. There was lots of green open space, and the main street was already dotted with flourishing businesses and trendy watering holes.

Still, despite all these obvious benefits, the opening felt more difficult to me right from the beginning and I think part of it was due to my changing role. Now that we were opening a new store, I had to take myself out of the day-to-day management of Logan Hardware, where I loved working, and that was hard for me. I loved working at that register, saying hello to everybody, being up close with our customer base, and working side by side with our team.

We promoted a dedicated sales associate named Drew as the inaugural manager to hold down the fort at Logan. Drew was also in recovery and set the bar higher for everyone who followed. He had a degree from UVA, Marc's alma mater, and the two of them liked to brag that this technically made them geniuses, a point I did not dare to argue. Drew was dedicated, professional and full of energy. He was also notoriously tardy, but that didn't bother us much as long as he got the job done.

With a newly minted leader, we were ready for the big move. The paperwork was signed, Ace and National Cooperative Bank were on board, and the shelving arrived right on time. I always get such a thrill seeing the first truck roll up, loaded with products to stock the shelves of a brand-new store. We had all learned by this point that we needed sturdy shoes, thick gloves, and an absurd number of box cutters to get a store ready. Lots of pizza and great music weren't a bad idea either.

We opened on a beautiful spring day in early March. The neighborhood window boxes of Glover Park were full of daffodils and tulips. The cherry blossoms, a Washington, DC treasure, were ready to burst all over town. I challenge anyone to visit DC in the spring and not think it is the most beautiful city in the country. We had unloaded, unpacked, sorted, and stocked over 100,000 pounds of shelving and product. I had been gliding through the days—high on adrenaline and pure positivity, and now the day was finally here to share it all with the world.

Getting the store ready to receive guests on day one is a whole different process from the set-up phase of the game. It's like throwing a housewarming party for hundreds of strangers. You're never completely ready. There is always something that you miss—one piece of laundry still swinging from the clothesline, a finger smudge on the windowpane—but guests are arriving and there is no time left for perfection. You have to throw open the doors and welcome the world as you are.

With the door set to open at 2:00, Marc's dad was still comically rushing around with a vacuum cleaner at 1:59. My parents drove in from Ohio with their car filled to the brim with bottles of cheap vodka and jugs of orange juice to ply our first-time guests at our screwdriver bar. We offered actual screwdrivers right alongside the drinkable kind.

Recipe from the Screwdriver Bar (mom not included)

Ingredients:

- Power drill
- Red Solo cups
- Ice
- Vodka (just regular old vodka, this is a Screwdriver bar no need to get fancy)
- Orange juice (no pulp)

Instructions:

Fill the paint can a quarter to a third of the way up with vodka. Throw in some orange juice and some ice. Put the lid on the can and shake thoroughly. Strain into shot glasses. Then put your power drill in the air and make it whirl as you do your shot.

Warning: do not operate the drill if you are also testing the screwdrivers

No one with half a brain cell, since the passage of workman's comp rules, would think that alcohol and power tools go together but the screwdriver bar was a hit. Our friend and loyal customer David Keifrider showed up wearing an Ace branded leather tool belt with its pockets full of shot glasses and bottles of booze. He wandered the aisles, trying to make friends while pouring shots for any brave shoppers willing to partake.

Yet, despite all our confidence going in, plus favorable press and neighborhood enthusiasm, we came away with the feeling that things hadn't gone off quite as well as we had wanted. We felt like we had to prove ourselves somehow, like we had to earn our customers' love. This was new for me and my whole staff. To be fair, the bar had been set pretty low for us in Logan Circle. Just the fact that we existed was good enough over there. Glover Park was different. The neighborhood expected something from us and we had to learn quickly what that something was and figure out how to deliver it.

I began paying more careful attention to our new customers. I stopped making assumptions about them based on their zip code. I began to ask myself some of the questions we should have asked in advance like, what is Glover Park like as a community? Who are these folks, and what do they need from us? How was Glover Park the same as Logan? How was it different? One of the first things I noticed was that there were dogs literally everywhere—and yet, there was no nearby pet store. The second thing I noticed is that there were lots and lots of children but no nearby toy store. This was a start.

The beauty of being a member of a cooperative like Ace is that there is flexibility built into the model if you choose to use it.

We added 200 pet products to our inventory mix and the kinds of things that kids love too. Soon our shelves were stocked with colorful tyke-sized gardening gloves, tiny dumpster trucks and garden tools scaled for kid-sized plots. I ran with my idea that if we sold what the neighborhood *needed*, then the neighborhood would need us back.

Ironically, we had our first close encounters with theft in stately Glover Park. It's not that we hadn't dealt with crime before. We had had the occasional shoplifter at Logan. And it is true that employee theft is an ongoing industry concern and one that retailers spend millions of dollars a year trying to thwart. We had contended with our share of that also.

As a company, we don't pretend theft does not exist, but we do choose to focus on the positive aspects of employee engagement. I tell our sales associates to focus on the 99% of the customers who are not shoplifting from us and I give the management team the same statistic as it relates to employees. Don't bury your heads, put best practices in place to safeguard from employee theft, but DO NOT dwell. Crime emerges from the most unlikely places, even in fancy Glover Park.

First there was Thomas, who was a 23-year-old college graduate, from an upper middle-class white family. He had parents who owned a small business in the mid-west. Thomas was hired on the spot, and we felt thrilled to have him. On paper, he was the ideal sales associate. He was personable, articulate, and very good with customers.

Thomas was the last person you would ever suspect of being a thief, but by the time we caught on, he had stolen thousands of dollars' worth of products from us. He was ordering through our system at reduced costs, then shipping the products to his parents to sell in their business. Maybe things that seem too good to be true usually are?

Then there was the septuagenarian tag team who managed to rob us blind and in slow motion to boot! Thinking back, it was kind of embarrassing. Video footage showed one old geezer using a blue picnic cooler to block the camera's view to the cash drawer while his partner snuck the key to the register out of the register drawer and into his pocket. It took about a year and a half for him to liberate that key with his shaky hand. And sure enough, a week later money went missing—chunks of it. These thieves moved at a glacial pace, but they were effective. Even as I write this, I feel the word amateur burning through the flesh on my forehead.

Rather than making us paranoid and cautious, my philosophy going forward after these incidents was to give up trying to guess who the thieves were. If two senior citizens with a picnic basket who looked like my grandma's best friends, or the wholesome, cornfed Thomases of the world were going to turn out to be crooks, then anyone could be a thief.

The neighborhood also had some preconceptions about us that were largely inaccurate. There were days when Jen, the manager, would call me crying, because a customer had called her useless. Or when William, a teammate and aspiring artist who drove his partner's Range Rover, was cornered by a customer who wanted to know *how he could afford a car like that*. Somebody even wrote an op-ed demanding that we accept checks from our customers because, after all, we weren't in a neighborhood "like Logan Circle anymore." It was clear that our team and the neighborhood needed to get to know each other a little better.

I believed passionately then and still believe now that a business leader needs to get out of the store and into the community. I was still actively involved with Logan Circle, so Jen began to fill that role in Glover Park. She even moved to the neighborhood, leased an apartment within walking distance of the store and truly became a part of the community—one of the neighbors. This had a tremendous impact on the business. It was really Jen who wiggled *our* way into the hearts and wallets of Glover Park. After that, the store become enormously profitable, and we started thinking about the next neighborhood.

Two of My Favorite Ace Stores

Cole Hardware in San Francisco began in the 1920s and has been in the Karp family since being purchased by patriarch Dave Karp in 1959.[17] Dave's son and grandson run the stores now and make urban hardware look so cool. I love so many things about how Rick and David operate but the window displays by team member Noelle are especially legendary.

Barnes Ace Hardware in Ann Arbor began in 1939 and is a staple in this bustling Michigan town. Three generations of Barnes family members have made this business into the flourishing and special place that it is. With thousands of houseware items, their Stadium Street store was an inspiration to me when I opened, proving that there is more than just tools in a successful hardware store.

Opening our second store in such a different neighborhood from our first and taught me that a cookie cutter approach won't work for all neighborhoods. They are as different and unique as the people who live there. If you are really going to understand where you are, first you have to drop your preconceptions. If you're going to build a mutually beneficial relationship that allows you both to thrive, you have to get past the surface with your neighbors, your customers, and your employees and really get to know one another.

NINE

Don't Judge Anyone by the Worst or Best Thing They've Ever Done

We hired Scott, or Skippy as we called him, after he had been clean for about six months and was still wearing a court-ordered ankle bracelet. He had gotten arrested for selling drugs, but it had been the wake-up call he had desperately needed.

I have gotten a lot of mileage talking about Skippy over the years. Who in their right mind hires a former drug dealer to "mind the store"? And who nicknames a guy like that *Skippy*? People often gasp when I tell them I hired him, but that's when I explain that the skillset that made Skippy so successful as a dealer also made him great in retail. There are three traits that made this former drug dealer an ideal candidate for us.

First, he was great with money—as in old-fashioned, cold hard cash. He was a pro at counting it, collecting it, and using it to buy new inventory.

Second, he was used to working odd hours—some people who need a dealer want them to be available outside of the 9 to 5. Skippy was used to working late, weekend hours, and every hour in between. On top of this, his house arrest only allowed him to leave for 12-step meetings or work, so he was always incredibly happy to have a place to go.

And third, he was fantastic with people. Especially difficult or occasionally dangerous people. I'm being unduly stereotypical here, but I would guess his previous customer base hadn't always been in the best mood, or very polite.

During his tenure, Skippy taught me more about customer service and about how to deal with excessively demanding shoppers or employees than any business book I've read. He started as a Sales Associate at Logan Hardware and eventually moved into a management role. By the time he was tapped to help us open store number three, we would have all but forgotten about his legal woes if it wasn't for the lagging court system that had backlogged the disposition of justice by about three years.

Skippy was facing a mandatory 11-year prison sentence but by the time his court date was set, he had already been clean for three years. While he was clocking thousands of hours in therapy, 12-step meetings and hard work, the court system was whirring away in the background, too overwhelmed to process his case. He often told me he felt he was caught in a perpetual spin cycle.

He had been working with us for two years, managing our third and by now busiest, location, when his case was finally called up for sentencing. By that time, it almost seemed like a moot point.

How do you take someone who is now a successful member of society and throw them into prison?

In 2015, it was the 100-year anniversary of making drugs illegal in the United States (the Harrison Narcotic Act came into effect in 1915[18]) and marked a century of bureaucratic delays, stigma and law enforcement issues that has only gotten worse over the years. Skippy's case was not unusual. It was representative of thousands of cases where citizens and families put their lives and their healing on hold, waiting for a court system that cannot seem to catch up.

Marc and I were asked to attend Skippy's final hearing as character witnesses. Along with members of Skippy's inner circle, we would be given a chance to speak about his personality and progress, his health and stability.

"He's drug free and happy," one witness said.

"He's been punished enough just playing the waiting game. He's done his time," said another.

This was a really tough day—there was so much at stake for Skippy. And I'll admit that while I was scared for him as a human being, selfishly, I also did not want to lose a great manager.

His sister cried the whole time she stood in front of the judge, her body wracked with sobs, as she tried to testify on behalf of her brother. I could tell the judge wasn't understanding a word and I worried that I would be just as emotional and unintelligible. Thank goodness my wonderfully composed husband Marc saved the day. He calmly and coherently told the judge that we run a respectable business that was thriving BECAUSE of Skippy. He explained that it would be a shame to remove a man from society when he was doing so well and contributing so much.

"Why should society foot the bill to lock up someone who has already reformed?" Marc asked the judge sensibly.

The judge looked like he agreed, but we couldn't be sure.

We held hands and our breath for what felt like eternity as the judge deliberated. Finally, he returned to the bench, looked at Skippy and said, "Get out of my courtroom, I never want to see you here again." The judge banged his gavel. Justice was done. Feeling a little shell shocked and beyond relieved, we all danced out of the courtroom.

Skippy was officially free from that day forward—with the expectation that he would remain clean and live a productive life. No more jewelry courtesy of the state monitored his movements. No court-ordered curfews scheduled his day. I will never forget the overwhelming feelings of joy and relief that enveloped us as we celebrated his second chance at life.

We were happy and grateful that we could keep growing with Skippy as one of our leaders. He helped us train a whole new generation of managers including African transplant Christinah who now runs our B2B program, selling to non-profits, businesses, and government agencies all over town. Christinah found us while at George Mason University completing her degree in International Affairs and Development and thankfully just never left. She absorbed Skippy's sage advice and passes it on whenever she can.

In 2006, Skippy moved over to manage our third location, about five miles from Logan Hardware, in a neighborhood that seemed a world away. Tenleytown is a buttoned-up neighborhood in Northwest DC made up of oversized rowhouses, stately single-family homes and sleepy side streets. Sidwell Friends, the private high school that has graduated more than one President's child is nearby, as is American University. We had chosen the neighborhood the same way we chose Glover—someone offered us a space. We thought: *Okay, this looks a little like Glover Park, practically right next door, no sweat. Let's do it!*

In order to afford a commercial lease in this swanky part of town we had taken over a portion of an underground parking garage, which 10 years prior had been witness to the demise of an 88-year-old home grown chain. Hechinger Hardware had been a beloved brand whose reputation still endured years after they had closed their doors. This gave us a real lift in the beginning. Still pining away for Hechinger's, residents enthusiastically accepted us as the heir apparent. Our revenue surpassed our first two locations within a year of opening. Marc likes to say, "We should have stopped at three" because the numbers were so comfortable during that time. We had no worries.

We called our team the "Subterraneans," like an underground colony of ants, we worked with no natural light or awareness of what the outside world was experiencing. Whether a violent hurricane or a whiteout blizzard was raging outside, it made little difference to us. The customers didn't seem to mind the bunker-like location and so we put our heads down and went to work building our third unique presence in the marketplace.

And then, on February 28th, 2007, less than a year after opening that store, I got a call that no business owner ever wants to receive.

"You've been held up. Robbed," the police officer on the line said dispassionately, and I shivered. The newly poured coffee I was holding immediately cooled. I wasn't worried about the merchandise; we pay copious amounts of insurance for that. But the officer told me that guns had been used and I retched, thinking of how my teammates must have felt in those terrifying moments. He explained that no one had been hurt but I knew the trauma must have been overwhelming. I could feel it seeping into my bones as if I had been there myself.

As the officer recounted the details, elsewhere a white Cadillac with gold rims went racing through the streets of our leafy new neighborhood, heading frantically toward what I assume was a less conspicuous part of town for such an 80s-inspired jalopy like that. Our tree-lined blocks were more accustomed to sleek BMWs or white Range Rovers. It might as well have had a sign on the grill that read "Out of Place."

The get-away driver was a teenage girl, barely out of high school with long braids and a look of steely determination on her face made her seem older than her years. She vainly attempted to steer her way out of the inevitable rush hour traffic that clogged the streets at 8:30 every weekday morning. She veered off Wisconsin Ave, leaving the main commercial corridor, disappearing into a tangle of residential side streets.

Riding shotgun and in the seat behind her sat her 33-year-old twin brothers, who had just sealed their fate by holding up our hardware store at gun point for 1,100 lousy bucks.

Video footage from a few days' prior showed the trio wandering around the store—obviously casing the place for safes, security cameras and a clean exit path. The surveillance tape shows them making their way slowly past expensive power tools, wandering our plumbing and electrical aisles, and winding their way farther and farther into the store until they ended up near the loading dock where they must have noted how they would make their getaway.

One week later, at approximately 7:45 a.m. and prior to the store opening, one of the twins, wearing a black ski mask, ambushed an employee taking the trash out the back door. He pushed the steel shaft of a gun into my teammate's back and forced him to walk to the cash registers while his twin brother followed behind. The car with the young driver remained idling in the back alley. It was a terrifying scene to contemplate.

They had obviously been focused on the cold hard cash because on the long march from one end of the store to the other, they passed tens of thousands of dollars' worth of power tools and equipment that would have been just as easy to load up and definitely more rewarding for them given the ultimate outcome. They made four of my employees lay on the ground in the office with guns pointed at their heads while they robbed the register.

The police showed up to find the entire staff, including Marc who had rushed across town to get to our team, chain smoking cigarettes in the back alley—one officer, trying to lighten the mood, asked if smoking was a prerequisite for working at our company. It took several nerve-wracking hours before they collected all the evidence and the information they needed and packed up and left the scene. Passersby peered in the front door like we were a human aquarium. The police put out an all-points bulletin search for the getaway car but had not heard anything at that point about the white Caddy lost in the winding lanes of Tenleytown.

At some point, the Cadillac turned down the wrong sleepy side street and ran right into unsuspecting Detective Andy Solberg, Head of the 2nd Precinct, who was pulling out of a parking spot and heard the alarm bells sound. The driver slammed on the brakes and they all jumped out and made a run for it as Detective Andy approached.

Only the teenage driver got away. With the help of an overhead patrol helicopter, the police cruisers managed to catch the twins. They were arrested, and ultimately sentenced to 12 years in prison. I remember feeling so sorry for their mother in court that day. She had raised twin sons only to lose them both on the same day.

This was not the sort of thing I had signed up for when I launched a little hardware business. It was just made crystal clear that we were not playing store anymore. Things just got real. The unimaginable had happened and we had to become more deliberate in our security practices. We had to protect our team, our money and our product, in that order.

We got past that incident and began to document stronger procedures. Skippy was the manager at the time and while he wasn't there during the robbery, he was our rock. He helped his team overcome the event and move past the heinous security breach.

And then, in 2014, after being on our team clean and sober for over 10 years, Skippy took me to breakfast and told me that he had started using again.

My fork froze midair halfway to my mouth. I could hear him speaking but the words refused to register.

"I've already stopped," Skippy reassured me. "And it won't happen again, Gina, I promise. But I wanted to tell you. I thought it was important that there were no secrets between us."

In that moment, I really wanted to believe him, so I did. We went back to eating breakfast, chatting about the team and future plans. Unfortunately, unbeknownst to me, he was high that very morning, but I was blinded by my love for him and I didn't see it. We all see mostly what we want to see. We all love in the way we must in order to get through another day. We all resort to a level of denial, whether we acknowledge it or not.

About three weeks after his "sort of" confession at the diner, we had to terminate Skippy for working under the influence. Rather than requiring him to go into rehab immediately, we had trusted him enough to have the strength to stop on his own accord. We had asked only that he subject himself to biweekly drug tests if he wanted to continue working for us. When he couldn't pass the tests, we had to let him go.

This was such a low point for me as a leader, and as Skippy's friend. There was a pit in my stomach and a dull ache in my head that I know now was a level of stress that I hadn't yet experienced up to that point. Nothing seemed to make it go away and frankly for a while, I wasn't sure if I could recover from this devastating violation of my trust. But of course, I did because what other choice was there?

When you're in the recovery hardware business, you must recover. Plus, we had grown large enough to become about a lot more than Skippy. I had a responsibility now for many lives, remaking themselves day by day in our aisles. I wasn't going to let Skippy stop that good work. He wouldn't have wanted us to. And so, we carried on and we remembered Skippy for the many good things he had brought to our aisles.

Despite his human shortcomings, Skippy's legacy has lived on in our culture like a beacon. Opening the Tenleytown store and working with Skippy allowed us to create a set of core values that we follow faithfully to this day. And I learned them all from a former drug dealer, who knew more about people than most of us ever will.

Marc asked me once where my faith in people came from. He knows I'm not a spiritual person but at my very core, I can see the good in every single human I meet. To me, finding good people means finding the good *in people*. Marc likes to say that "You can't judge anyone by the worse or best thing they've ever done." I fell in love with the good inside Skippy as soon as we met. That's a choice that, no matter what happened, I will never regret.

TEN

You're Better Than You Think You Are

had a dream once where I was seated in an enormous theater. The space was cavernous with thousands of red plush seats and a soaring, gilded ceiling. As the theater lights dimmed a hush came over the crowd. A tall man in a tuxedo walked through an opening in the long velvet curtains and took center stage. Then he walked ominously toward the audience pointing at the person seated immediately in front of me.

"You're a fake!" he bellowed, and then pointed to another person. "You're a fake," he said again, and then pointed at another, and another, with the same damning resolve. Finally, I looked around and realized that the entire audience looked exactly like me. I was occupying every seat in the house. I was having the actor's nightmare, only my theatre was a hardware store.

I've spent 18 years fighting imposter syndrome. I can be surrounded by friends yet look around the table and think: *How the hell did I get here? Do people think I know what I'm talking about?* I didn't become comfortable enough to claim my authority until I joined the Ace Hardware Board of Directors.

Marc and I moved out of Logan Circle in 2006 because we needed a break. We had left behind the "group home" that had sustained us while we built the business. One of the ways we had afforded to eat while building the business was to stuff our house with friends who helped pay the mortgage. It was a friendly and revolving cast of characters, who lent the air of a small-town motel to the joint.

Margie came for a year and infused us with her funny sayings like *Shot who?* (Excuse me, what did you say?) or *Good groceries!* (Holy cow!). Lisa passed through on her way out west and Christine made a second appearance living with us in between stints in Uganda or grad school until she finally went to work for USAID. There were others, all of them loved by us in a variety of ways and at that age who doesn't appreciate a perpetual pajama party? We were surrounded by buddies ready to chug wine with us at all hours. It was a wayward house, a crash pad, and our ticket to grow. And then, eventually, we outgrew the place. We were ready for some privacy.

Our new home was about three quarters of a mile down the road in a neighborhood called Penn Quarter, about five blocks from the White House. Marc liked to joke that we "should invite Barack and Michelle over for dinner because technically we're neighbors."

For a time, I affectionately called our condo the cocoon, because that's what it felt like. There wasn't a lot of natural light, so it was dark and womb-y. Our minuscule balcony overlooked the dimly lit alley that had provided the escape route for John Wilkes Booth after he shot Lincoln. Finally, we weren't surrounded by customers. No one knew who we were and that allowed us some room to exhale. We were just two anonymous faces on the DC tourist route, and it was nice and peaceful to be out of the neighborhood limelight.

Life-changing opportunities were starting to emerge for me thanks to the hardware industry and I was excited about that. I wanted to make the most of everything that was crossing my path. By that point we had four locations and I had started to venture outside of our four walls a bit more—first into our immediate store communities and then into the rest of the country. Most significantly, 2007 was the year that I got the call to join the Ace Board of Directors, changing the trajectory of my whole life and amplifying my voice in many important ways.

However, when that fateful phone call rang through, I wasn't sure I was ready. I was in our condo just hanging out watching TV with Marc when James Hatcher called. James was a retailer in Richmond, Virginia whose business has a tagline I have always loved: *"Pleasants Hardware: Most Anything Since 1915."* I think that perfectly sums up a good hardware store in just a couple of words.

"Hi Gina," he said, his voice friendly and cheerful, and one, with all its southern nuance, that I would come to know much better in years to come. "I'm calling because Rick Karp from San

Francisco put your name into the hat for the upcoming board election."

I was speechless. Stunned silent. At first, I thought that James must be joking, but he wasn't.

"Rick thought you might be interested. Are you? Interested, I mean? Gina?"

I paused for as long as I could, but then couldn't contain my excitement any longer. I began jumping up and down like a little kid. I know, it was incredibly unprofessional, but I was young, and I just never expected anybody to ask me to be on the board of any company let alone a national one. I was so honored and then of course, immediately felt like a fake. Surely, they didn't realize who they had picked. There must have been some mistake. I was way too green for this enormous responsibility. What were they thinking?

James explained a little bit of the rationale behind my nomination, and I realized that asking me to join the Board did make sense for them on a certain level. Lori Terpstra, the only woman on the board was stepping down soon, along with Rick, who was the lone voice for the urban market stores. I checked both of those boxes. So what if I lacked any board experience? I hadn't known anything about running hardware stores before I opened one, and that was working out okay. So, I agreed to be interviewed and began the process of becoming the third woman and youngest person to ever serve on the Ace Corporate Board of Directors.

Most new board members have at least two interviews, vetting sessions where existing members suss out warts and intelligence levels. I often think that had I gone through the traditional process, there is no way in hell I would have been chosen. They would have figured out before it was too late that I wasn't ready and that I'm somebody with strong opinions that I can't keep to myself.

My transition from member of the co-op to member of the board could have probably gone more smoothly. I had a very short runway. When my number was drawn, I just had to take off and gain altitude quickly. I was treated to a couple hours of orientation and a helpful comment from the General Counsel who told me, "Don't dwell on the no votes, Gina. Those guys just don't want a woman on the board."

Members are elected for three-year terms and can be re-elected twice to serve up to nine years and usually do, assuming they don't royally screw up. Historically, board members come from multi-generational retail hardware families, born with power tools in their blood. In other words, folks who were nothing like me.

Meetings are held four times a year in Oak Brook, Illinois and despite only being about 20 miles from downtown Chicago, it felt like a world away from the big city. The company headquarters is near the original McDonald's University which was also home to a beautiful midcentury modern hotel where we were housed for our visits for most of my nine-year tenure. My first couple of meetings were terrifying—after years of being attached to my business at the hip I had come untethered. I found myself in a board room with no ability to even glance at my phone. During our breaks I would hide in a bathroom stall and frantically try to catch up with home while simultaneously keeping an eye on the ticking clock. Eventually I enjoyed the time apart, but it took me a year to become comfortable with the distance. I was on *Ace time* now and would learn to devote these precious hours to the members I was elected to represent.

The meeting structure was strict—pages and pages of documentation were sent out in advance and the schedule was set in stone. There was little wiggle room and most of the serious conversations happened after hours when we were at dinner or the hotel bar. For someone used to running the show and talking all day long, it was rough. I had to bite my tongue, sit on my hands, and tug on my hair to stop myself from asking too many questions or piping in with my opinion a little too often. Eventually, though, a rhythm emerged, and I like to think I adapted to the cadence. I never got accustomed to being the lone outspoken voice, however.

At first, I would feel my evil imposter twin raising her head, reminding me that I was a fake. Usually never at a loss for words, I would become a deer in the headlights in these moments and couldn't weigh in. My insides would tremble, my brain completely frozen. I would shoot fervent glances at a friend across the table, silently pleading that he or she would agree with what I was saying or make me feel a little less alone.

One chairman liked to refer to me as *passionate,* but he used it in a way that I found a little insulting—he might as well have said you're *so emotional, we men don't do business like that.*

One member called me a broken record on the subject of diversity when I continued to bring it up at every single meeting. I would be lying if I told you neither of these experiences made me mad. I'm well aware of the chips I carry around on my shoulders. But I had already had lots of practice with negativity—I processed these sorts of comments like those from the naysayers about my teammates. They just fueled my resolve to keep going.

I did feel like a round peg in a sea of square holes most of the time, which is never fun, but I just could not make myself give up. Eventually, some of my friends were also elected to the board. My peer group was catching up to me and I was so relieved, thinking that, finally, I would be surrounded by friends and allies. Unfortunately, what I discovered was that not even my friends would stand behind me when I'd speak out on sensitive issues. I learned that not everyone was a big mouth like me, and not everyone is brave.

My experience on the board, even the difficult moments, taught me an important lesson in being uncomfortable. Most of us avoid discomfort like the plague but once you've endured it you realize it's not that bad. It won't kill you. And since change and growth is always going to involve some discomfort, it's a good thing to understand that you can survive it.

Being a Great Board Member

Unlike corporate boards, women have served on non-profit boards forever. I've learned there are three significant ways to contribute to them:

- 🔵 *Wealth*—how can you financially contribute with your own money or connect the organizations to others?

- **Work**—do you have the time and energy to run programs or put in (wo)man hours that the organization could benefit from?
- **Wisdom**—do you have a particular knowledge base or skill set that the organization needs such as legal skills or marketing expertise?

This experience also gave me the opportunity to look at my own business in a broader context. I gained an appreciation for how a multi-billion-dollar company operates amid so many opposing voices. One member called it the "joy of the co-op." Thousands of us all going in different directions—begging for support but ignoring well intended advice. I've certainly been guilty of this over the years. No one wants a big brother until she desperately *needs* a big brother. In its own way, Ace had been and still is that big brother, annoying at times, but ready to catch you when you fall.

So many times, I left those meetings feeling like an utter failure. I hadn't gotten along or played along—and I hoped to God it wasn't as bad as I remembered it in my mind afterward. Every scene would replay in my mind—a movie on rewind and forward and then rewind again, and I often wished that I could go back in time and rewrite the script.

I was sure everyone talked—er, complained about me the second we all parted ways and I couldn't shake the feeling that I had spent two days banging my head against the wall for nothing. When I look back now though, I realize, I am proud of my Board service, and it taught me a lot.

Glennon Doyle says, "There's one thing worse than sticking up for what you believe in, and that's not sticking up for anything at all." I didn't have to worry about that. No matter how much I might cringe after a meeting, I'd wake up the next day and do the same damn thing. My convictions outweighed my fear and embarrassment. When it comes to social injustice, I have little tolerance and even less of a filter.

I have come to realize that not everyone is built this way, and I'm not sure I have come to grips with that, even now. I have learned that most people just aren't willing to put their money where their mouth is. Most people aren't brave. But more of us could be, if we tried a little harder at it, and realized how great it feels to stand up for others, and for the principles you believe in.

I knew I had a responsibility. I was in a position to use my voice to speak for some of my constituency in that co-op, a constituency of women and urban owners that didn't get heard at the table very often. Thinking about them helped me feel more comfortable about being outspoken. So, I poked and prodded until Ace sanctioned the launch of a group we named "Ace Women in Retail."

Ace Women in Retail is an affinity group whose mission is to educate and elevate the women who work in hardware, many of whom told me they had never felt heard before. What started out as a gathering of approximately 30 attendees soon grew to more than 100 members, with meetings at our biannual national conventions. I walked into that first gathering of ours with my heart full and my expectations exploding. I wasn't sure if the event would grow legs, but I knew that for at least one convention we were out of the shadows and Ace was finally forced to notice.

Female store owners, store managers and members of the Ace Corporate staff looked around and marveled at a room full of beautiful female faces at a show devoted to hardware. Several hardware affiliates around the country have women's groups now and it's not as uncommon for women to be spotlighted in hardware media. I know our efforts at Ace have helped to make this happen. Thanks to our work, the next generation of women won't have to feel so alone out on that limb.

Strong women have always been my guiding angels. When I moved to Logan Circle, I met dozens of fiercely proud urbanites, so many of them women, who helped rebuild the neighborhood. When our neighbor in Logan Circle, community pioneer Connie Maffin passed away, a group of us named ourselves the Logan Ladies and gathered together to celebrate Connie's legacy. She had taught us to take care of each other.

Elizabeth, like Connie, took a chance on selling real estate in Logan Circle when others wouldn't even walk there, and has reaped the benefits. Frona, her partner in crime, is over 70 and still jumps out of helicopters to ski. I think of these women as my cheerleading squad and role models. I can only hope to be as important in someone's lives as these ladies have been in mine.

At such a pivotal time as a young business owner, my board experience, and these North Star ladies in my life taught me that I had to look outside of my lane in order to find inspiration and grow. I needed unlikely mentors which meant looking in unlikely places. Oddly enough, I didn't have to look any farther than milk farmers. Yes, as in cows. Roberta MacDonald came into our lives with the ferocity of a tornado, whipping up everything around her like the butter her cooperative members at Cabot Creamery churned and sold. Holy cow (pun intended), has she taught me a lot about venturing outside my lane. Principle #6 in co-op speak is "Cooperating with Other Cooperatives," and when Roberta and her team from Cabot randomly contacted us in 2014 to ship us cheese from Vermont for one of our events, we were hooked.

Cabot is a cooperative made up of 1,500 family-owned farms in New England. In addition to making some of the best cheese in the US, they support any other cooperative in the country willing to accept their creamy generosity. Their marketing budget has created innovative programs like the Gratitude Grill and Random Acts of Cheddar. For a couple of years, they awarded 50 community volunteers a spot on a five-day cruise and Marc and I were privileged to be included. While on board they asked their attendees to wear a green satin sash with the word Celebrity on it to pique the interest of the other ocean-going guests. Of course that idea worked, and we immediately had an excuse to talk to everybody about the farmers of the Cabot cooperative. There is a reason why I have looked up to Roberta for so long, she's a marketing genius.

My delight at being chosen as one of the invited guests was far outshined by the inspiring people I met on board, such as Dwight Owens. Dwight was paralyzed in a drunk driving accident when he was young, and he now spends his life speaking to and educating people about the dangers of drinking and driving. His messages of resilience despite his life in a wheelchair are an inspiration for any age.

The cruise culminated with all of us dancing the night away at a silent disco. Dozens of passionate and noisy community activists who use our voices daily to speak for others went silent, gyrating to the beats playing in our own ears—perhaps a reminder that we don't always have to use our actual voice for amazing connections to happen.

An old retailer once called me a shameless self-promoter for seeking publicity for my little business. Roberta taught me that's a bunch of BS. If I don't talk about my team and our stores, who will?

So, there are my building blocks—hardware, women and cheese. I have always loved the concept of businesses "doing well, while doing good," and through the help of the many and diverse guiding lights in my life, I started to figure out how to make money AND make our corner of the world a better place to live and work. We're not doing anything new. The guy at Toms Shoes goes before us. As do Ben & Jerry and Jane Fonda. She launched an entire exercise video market because she needed to raise money for The Campaign for Economic Democracy, founded by her second husband. Maybe it's not as sexy, but why couldn't cleaning supplies and paint brushes do the same for me and the causes I believe in?

We might be small, but our efforts are not. We have never wanted to be guilty of waiting *for someone else* to provide the solution. I used to find myself saying, "I just run a hardware store"—the imposter in me refusing to see that what we do is important. I now know that it's okay to tell my team that what we do is more than *just* run a hardware store. Much more. And every time we speak up for a worker, a fellow co-op member or a fellow small business owner, especially when it's hard, we learn that we are better than we thought we were.

ELEVEN

You Can't Control the Wind, but You Can Adjust Your Sails

My **strong desire** to grow jobs was propelling me to open more locations, but without the seaworthy and occasionally salty Captain John, I don't think we would ever have ventured into Baltimore. When Baltimore comes up in conversation, nine times out of 10 the 2002 HBO series *The Wire* is mentioned next. For 60 episodes, the network shone a spotlight on every negative stereotype associated with Charm City and no one, it seems, can forget it. When asked at one point if he wanted to expand there, Marc responded, "The only way you'll find me in Baltimore is if I'm in prison."

Baltimore gets a bum rap. It is in many ways a model American City—having reinvented itself over and over as transportation and technological advancements evolved over centuries. Industrialization led to the development of major roads, a robust shipping industry and the expansion of the railroad system.[19] A steady influx of immigrants from Poland, Italy and Ireland, along with large African American and Jewish communities helped create a melting pot of ideas.[20] By 1893, Baltimore had more millionaire philanthropists than any other city in the United States and they left their imprint in the form of institutions like Johns Hopkins, the Walters Art Museum, and countless others.[21]

Tragedy struck in 1904, when downtown Baltimore burned to the ground. The fire consumed 140 acres, destroyed 1,526 buildings, and burned 2,500 companies out of their offices.[22] Not to be deterred, the city's business district was rebuilt better within three years.[23]

Baltimore is a city of hope, passion, and bootstrapping, which are the traits that most of us don't see when our only glimpse is through the lens of a TV drama. By the time Captain John suggested that we open a store there, several Baltimore neighborhoods were experiencing an urban renewal, much like the rest of the country. Young people, retirees, and families with young children, were moving into and reclaiming communities, adding their own flair. If that does not play into the concept of recovery, I'm not sure what does. For us, Baltimore became just another place that felt like home.

When we met Captain John in late 2005, he was clean, sober, and tremendously overqualified to work as a sales associate. He was attempting to make a go at being a mortgage broker during the beginning of one of the biggest housing crises in American history and things weren't going so well. The United States housing bubble was about to burst with a total of 1.2 million foreclosures filed in 2006[24] and John was stuck in a dead-end career. Like many serial entrepreneurs however, going back to work "for the man" was not an option. He needed something to do to bide his time until he planned out his next adventure and someone told him to come see us.

Prior to meeting us, John had built a successful nightclub and bar business in Washington. John's club was one of the coolest spots on the circuit, a place to see and be seen.

John had cultivated a loyal following and built his success through his magnetic personality, all the while swearing to himself that he would never be one of *those* bar owners, the kind who got drunk at their own bar. That lasted about a year until a boyfriend introduced him to cocaine and all that changed for a while. As if that wasn't enough of a challenge to overcome, the bar burned down one night, and it sent John and his business partners into a tailspin. Hospitalized for stress and unsure how to go on with life, Captain John's North Star status took a nosedive. He told me that the wind changed direction that day and he went from popular to pariah in the blink of an eye.

I remember how happy I was from the very first day Captain John came into the picture. He was like a breath of fresh air on an open sea. If I am being honest, John was probably the first true professional retailer we had on our staff. Sure, we had hired others with retail experience, but John was different. He reset the bar for us.

John started as a Sales Associate, quickly became an Assistant Manager, and then one day in late 2006, he called and said he had been thinking about moving to Baltimore. He explained that it was less expensive to live there, and he thought a fresh start outside of DC might do him some good. An avid sailor and nautical history buff, John longed to live on the water in a harbor town full of character and historical resonance. Baltimore was close and fit the bill perfectly. So, he wondered if we would be interested in expanding there with him as a partner.

Rules of Retail Expansion for Landlocked Sea Captains

⊙ Pick the right partner, because if things get tough, you want to know that your first mate isn't going to leave you adrift on an unfriendly sea

⊙ Have a good anchor, because sometimes it's a real benefit to be able to stay right where you are

⊙ Go where the competition isn't

⊙ Pick neighborhoods with strong identities and personalities

⊙ Make sure you're standing on solid ground

At the time, I didn't think it was such a leap of faith to go along with Captain John's plan. It wasn't that far outside of our regional comfort zone—but the naysayers in my world felt differently and didn't hesitate to tell me about it. The doubters and skeptics crawled out of the woodwork to tell us we were crazy or too trusting and guaranteed that we were definitely going to lose our shirts. I'm not sure what they were more concerned about, our partnership with Captain John, or the city of Baltimore itself.

We had heard every one of these arguments when we had expanded a few short miles across town, so we did what we did then: we ignored them all.

It wasn't long after our initial phone call that our Federal Hill outpost opened, with Captain John at the helm. We felt like urban pioneers again—paving the way for the Ace brand and local hardware in another great American city that needed a little renovating. There were over 600,000 people within the Baltimore City limits[25] and only two or three small hardware stores. How could we go wrong?

We have always operated on the philosophy that we wouldn't open a new store close to another locally owned hardware store. We didn't want to compete with other small local businesses. We started our search in Federal Hill, and while there was one funny old hardware place in the neighborhood, we decided to overlook it. The owner was not serious about much besides his fishing. He would close up shop on a random Tuesday if the fish were biting, so you were out of luck if your toilet stopped working. Or he would change prices to fit his whim so that a bolt might cost .35 one day and .65 the next. We weren't too worried about him.

The timing was right for a company like ours. It didn't feel like a risky stretch for us. It felt more like a grand new adventure. We had begun the process of documenting our company values, the principles we could neatly pack up for Captain John to take along with him when he opened far away. We also had the foundational elements of an HR program, something of a novelty in the hardware world at the time. What evolved was a wonderfully reciprocal relationship. We taught John the ins and outs of cooperative retailing and he taught us lessons in leadership that we still use to this day.

The Captain was less about lectures than he was about "all hands on deck." He believed in hard work, and he didn't have a lot of patience when it came to complainers. He had grown up in Chicago in a big Irish Catholic family and was used to straight talk. He liked to say, "Hey Gina, people should just be happy they have a job. Stop babying everyone!"

Captain John hired a workforce from the neighborhood, and they seemed to know everyone. He infused in them the value of being helpful—the code that we had built our reputation on. He also took a chance on people who needed one. Marc and I might have been far away on the day to day, but we celebrated when the store hit milestones and mourned when sad things happened, like when a young employee overdosed and died.

Federal Hill is located near the southern border of Baltimore. It has just under 35,000 residents[26] and includes the famous Inner Harbor. When we opened there, it was a little rough around the edges, but you could feel big things coming—it reminded us of Logan Circle. The community was made up of long-time residents and young newcomers looking for charming but inexpensive housing and Federal Hill did not disappoint. Many of the quaint row homes in the community are on the city's historic register and new developments were sprouting up everywhere.

Famous People from Our Baltimore Neighborhoods or very Near By

Our Baltimore neighborhoods have churned out, or have a connection to, some famous people, including some amazing authors. Maybe there is hope for me! Some on this list include:

- Michael Phelps famously devoured enormous breakfasts at Pete's Grille in Waverly while training for the Olympics.[27]

- Duff Goldman of Charm City Cake fame grew his empire in a building near our Waverly store.

- Jada Pinkett Smith is not shy talking about her less than glamorous life growing up in Balitmore City.[28]

- Hilton Carter got his BFA at the Maryland Institute College of Art in downtown Baltimore before becoming the influencer, tastemaker, and author that he is today.[29]

- Laura Lippman, a bestselling author, grew up in Baltimore and was a *Baltimore Sun* reporter for 12 years.[30]

- Bestselling author Tom Clancy grew up in Baltimore City and became one of the richest authors in the world.

Federal Hill is also near both of Baltimore's professional sports teams' stadiums, so the bar scene was lively and there were no shortages of places to grab a pint and burger. In the decade-plus that we've been in business there, countless retail establishments have come and gone—a revolving door that reflects the inexpensive commercial rent prices and the ease of taking a chance on a bright idea. But if your business has a beer tap and some bar stools, it's a good bet it's been there for ages.

The nondescript space we leased had once been a grocery store.

It was located at the southern end of Light Street, one of the main thoroughfares in the neighborhood. It had about 8,000 square feet and even a small parking lot. It also represented an uncharacteristic hiccup of fear on our part. The building was for sale OR lease and we chose to lease it; we were obviously not 100% comfortable with our newly hatched experiment. Two or three years in, we asked the landlords if it was still available to purchase. Their response was, "No way! You're too timely with your rent payments." Apparently, they had finally found responsible tenants and we learned an important lesson about what you might lose when you hesitate.

Our stomachs fell in love with Baltimore too. Something about Federal Hill makes us want to eat the minute Marc and I jump in the car to drive there. We will barely cross the DC/Maryland line before one of us asks, "What's for lunch?" and we start to tick off the options. World-famous crab cake sandwiches, piping hot French fries, fried oysters, fried pickles (fried everything), great pastries—YUM. Each visit is a feast of mega calories just waiting to happen.

Traffic at our new location grew slowly, but the community was supportive and we saw many of the same faces daily. It felt like an old-fashioned neighborhood where everybody knew everybody and looked out for each other. We even had our very own beat cop on the block. One afternoon, he dragged a shoplifter with a bag full of stolen items back to our store insisting that he return the items and apologize.

Rules for Stopping Shoplifters

Retailers unfortunately lose millions and millions of dollars a year to shoplifters, and everyone is always trying to build a bigger mousetrap (no pun intended). The money we lose could be used to lower prices, raise wages or bring in new items to entice local shoppers. Over the years, we've learned two primary rules that guide how we deal with this issue:

Rule #1—Good customer service. It has been proven repeatedly that the best deterrent to shoplifting is great customer service. If people do not feel invisible, they are less compelled to steal.

Rule #2—There is no Rule #2. Beyond Rule #1, there isn't much you can do.

Captain John had been right, Baltimore was a wonderful city for us, and soon, we found ourselves looking for a second location. We settled on a neighborhood about four miles north of Federal Hill called Waverly. On paper, Waverly seemed like a poor choice for a hardware store in some pretty major ways. For example, the average household income was roughly $50,000 less than it had been in our previous locations. Gritty, forlorn, and a little rough around the edges, Waverly, however, spoke to me from the very start. The building itself is an old post office that was built in 1931 at a time when architecture was grander than it is today. Designed in the Beaux Arts style with enormous, curved windows, and a beautiful gray brick, it doesn't look like a hardware store. The inside is not as pretty as the façade but still adds character and flair to everything that we sell, and we have never wanted polished, perfect spaces anyway.

Despite having spent little time there, Waverly Ace Hardware on Homestead Street holds a special place in my heart. It quickly became evident that my love for the location would translate into dollar signs because the community showed up and supported us in all the right ways. Thanks to its proximity to Johns Hopkins University, Waverly is wonderfully diverse in both people and housing stock.

Lots of old houses mean something is always breaking. The neighborhood is full of old secret warehouses, successful entrepreneurs and a funky old diner where Michael Phelps famously ate thousands of pancakes while in training. Hope and perseverance live side by side in a neighborhood that has grown TV personalities and Olympians—all evidence that anything can happen.

Opening day at that store was a comedy of errors. We had a big event planned and were ready to show off our shiny new space when the power and the internet went out. A transformer or something had blown in the neighborhood, so we had to welcome our guests into a poorly lit store. We hand wrote our sales slips because the cash registers were rendered useless. We might have all panicked a little bit, but fortunately, no one cared. They were just happy that we had arrived, and it certainly was a unique opening that people wouldn't soon forget.

Of course, the businesses in Baltimore did present their various challenges, some much more serious than others. The Waverly store was robbed at gun point four times. The glass windows and glass doors were shattered by midnight thieves on several occasions and Captain John spent countless hours in the middle of the night talking with the police after the alarms were set off. I always envisioned him in his pajamas and slippers calmly showing a detective the security footage and offering any clues that might have gone unnoticed.

Thanks to years sailing solo, Captain John knew how to face down a storm with perfect poise. And he never abandoned his ship, not even once. I would never have been able to return to the scene of those crimes every day so my admiration for John grew with each incident. We weren't physically there to help him or provide instant support and that always made me feel guilty. But he was tough, with a resolve to always reopen for the guests who did NOT want to steal or rob us. I don't remember John ever saying that he wanted to give up or move locations or even close the place down. All of this only reinforced that we had chosen the right partner who could weather a storm with the best of them.

Perhaps the funniest part about this store is that it is always sort of a mess. Despite having great leaders and young energetic team members, keeping it tidy and well merchandised hasn't always been a focus. It's hard for me to care though when the garden center we built after six years has become a wonderland of greenery in an urban desert and has even won "Best Garden Center in Baltimore."[31] Whether it's smart or not, we always say that good revenue makes up for bad habits.

Captain John retired in 2019 and the stores are still going strong thanks to the strong foundation he laid for us. Today, John is living his dream, sailing the costal waterways of America aboard a 1979 DeFever Trawler named *Morning Prayer*, with his First

Mate, his cat Princess by his side.

Bring on the Cats

At some point we realized that store cats could serve a work function by scaring away the mice but not the guests, and they became quite a colorful addition to the culture of our stores. The charismatic rescues Ben, Decker, and Dapper stroll around our three Baltimore stores like they own the joint, and they have lots of friends who come in just to say hello to them.

Named after vendors Benjamin Moore, Black + Decker, and DAP Products, our felines have Facebook pages with thousands of fans and their own product line of socks and buttons. I once asked our marketing manager to leave them out of our promotions because I wasn't sure we were allowed to have store cats and the very next day the Baltimore Sun ran a story about one of them on the front page of the newspaper. So much for anonymity.

I learned so many things from Captain John about hard work, about accountability, about staring into the eye of a storm, and keeping your sails open. I learned what grace means, why the chance to start over is such a gift, and how bread, cast upon the water, returns a hundred-fold.

TWELVE

It's the Times In Between That Count

A **sage hardware store** owner once told me that the bigger you get, the more likely you are to suffer a failure. He meant that the more stores we opened, the more likely it was that one of them just wouldn't work.

No one wants to think about business failure, however, especially as an inevitability, so I pushed it to the far reaches of my mind and marched forward. We had it all figured out. How could we possibly fail?

In 2009, we were planning our fifth location and my ego had me convinced that everything we did turned to gold—or at least some approximation of it. These days the phrase "You have to earn your luck" is taped to my computer monitor. But back then, I thought we had banked enough success that everything was just going to work from here on out. No luck needed. Marc and I can look back with good laughs at mistakes we made or the things we didn't know at various points in time but I'm not sure it had occurred to me back then that something might legitimately *not work*.

We had three important criteria we always tried to honor when choosing a new location.

We looked for neighborhoods with a name. Logan Circle, Glover Park, Takoma Park, Waverly. We have come to realize throughout the years that a proud, recognized name is synonymous with a strong community, no matter the demographics or average household income.

In addition to a name, the neighborhood needed to have a strong identity—Logan Circle set the gold standard for this. It was a neighborhood that had a personality that was palpable. It had real character and vision, a raw energy that anyone living there could feel, and a growing population determined to grow a strong sense of *place*.

Finally, and probably most importantly, there has to be a desire to *shop local*. More than just rehabbing houses, we want our communities to want to support local businesses. We want customers who, like us, do not want to get into their cars to run errands. We like walkers—people who stop in on their morning AND afternoon dog walks and want to congregate on sidewalks with their neighbors.

How can we know this about a place? Well, in Logan Circle for example, the Community Association voted three to one against letting a Starbucks open in the neighborhood. The association had no real say in the matter, but the landlord was interested in how his new tenant would be perceived and was nice enough to ask for the vote. The introduction of a national chain—a global brand—was not something we were ready to allow into our budding commercial district.

When we opened in 2003, Ace Hardware had less-strict brand standards and putting the word ACE in our name and on our building was not a requirement. In fact, that didn't come about until 2006 or so. We purposefully left Ace out of our local brand name because we knew everyone would see Ace and think *corporate*. It began our practice of naming our stores after the neighborhoods we inhabited because it helped underline the neighborhood's local pride. We wanted people to know that although we were part of a co-op, we were first and foremost, an independently owned and operated neighborhood hardware store, which is also pretty cool.

It was with these guiding principles written boldly on our clipboards that we opened our fifth Washington location in 2008 at 1055 5th Street NW and managed to ignore every single one of them.

This neighborhood did not have a name, identity, a community association, or any local stories that neighbors gossiped with each other about in front of their local hardware store, mini-mart or pub. There were no local stores or stories. Everything was new, just waiting for community to happen.

We named the store 5th Street Ace Hardware after the street because it wasn't a "real" neighborhood yet and we plowed forward like nothing was wrong. We opened with all the usual milestones in their proper order—press releases, opening sales, and community announcements. We did the whole nine yards, just like always. The residents we interacted with were happy to see us and we had plenty of positive feedback. No red flags ran up the flagpole. We were ready to coast in the fast lane.

And then we opened and the enthusiasm ground to a halt. Sales were painfully slow. That whole first year, sales were about a quarter of what we had forecast. We didn't panic right away. The banking and start-up types all say that you should expect a new venture to take two or three years to turn a profit. So, even though this pace was very different to that at our first four locations, we blew it off as a hiccup in our trajectory.

"Give it a little more time!" I would say to our worried manager. "You're doing all the right things, it will turn around." To our leadership team, and by that point to myself as well, "The neighborhood is still new. They'll find us."

Over the years, I've been accused of leading by "cheerocracy" and it's true. I am guilty of living in a place full of exclamation points. I believe it's good to maintain some cheer when you're losing money every day. The one person I wasn't saying anything to was Marc. It was as if a dam was keeping a deluge of unspoken negatives held back.

But it didn't take long for Marc to raise concerns, and these started with the property owners. Landlords often remain faceless entities, sinister behemoths looming somewhere unseen, waiting to pounce. This *us versus them* mentality that can sometimes be unfair, was in this case 100% true. They had already started to demonstrate a degree of shadiness that had Marc on high alert. Their grandiose plans for fully leased retail space were not materializing. There were still vacant store fronts on and around our block, and that certainly didn't help with our foot traffic.

The building did contain a new Safeway which at the time was very exciting. Large swaths of DC had long been known as food deserts. Residents had to travel long distances on buses or the Metro to get to anything that resembled fresh food. If you wanted to stay in the neighborhood, there was a 7-Eleven or corner bodega—nothing says nourishing and delicious meal prep like a Slurpee. But even with the advent of the much-celebrated grocery store, our sales were moving at a glacial pace. Heading into year two, our delusional landlords still insisted on their inflated rent—we were paying $38,000 a month and Marc and I both had to start facing some facts about the lack of revenue growth.

Marc made the first telling observations about our location. He noticed that all the new residents seemed to be up and coming—young people in their late 20s or early 30s who worked for the tech industry in the suburbs and commuted out of town every day. Or maybe they worked on the Hill and had no money or time to fix, decorate or renovate their homes. Their apartments were new, and most were rentals. Even if they wanted to renovate, they weren't allowed to.

We knew what the neighborhood was lacking—what amenities residents were leaving our block to buy, and we started stocking those items, but for some reason, it wasn't translating into revenue streams for us. Nothing was working, and I started thinking back to the early days in our very first store, when everything seemed to be going our way. Everything we had touched had turned to gold. What had changed? What was different now? And then I remembered Bryan.

When Bryan showed up in my life, he was in the throes of chemotherapy, was in recovery, and had recently gotten out of prison. He was convinced that there was no one on earth who would give him a job, so I did.

In his interview, he told me that he had gotten clean in prison and hadn't come within an inch of using since then. He worked with us for almost a year, becoming an integral part of the beating heart of Logan Hardware, and became embedded in mine. He was probably the first employee we hired who had actual DIY experience and when he provided advice to our customers, it was the real deal. That year ended abruptly one day, however, when Bryan went back out. That term "back out" is used to describe when someone starts using drugs again, and the expression makes me so incredibly sad. Words that were supposed to mean something exhilarating or impressive like "Let me tell you about my friend who "went *back out* into the world to do amazing things" or "I *went back* out into the world, full of pride" or something like that. But Bryan went back out and was found under a park bench four days later. He was brought back to our house to sleep off his drug-induced stupor while his friends figured out what to do with him.

For three days and two nights, my house reverberated with the soundtrack of a terrifying horror film. Honestly, I never want to experience that again. The effects of meth on a person last from 6–12 hours on average, depending on how much has been consumed and how it was administered (IV, oral, etc.).[32] Meth has a half-life of 9–24 long, gruesome hours,[33] and that only reduces the amount of meth in a person's blood by half. Meth can be detected in the blood for up to three days and in the hair follicles for up to 90 days.[34]

Bryan screamed and moaned and screamed some more as the drugs left his body, an exorcist to breathe life back into the body of my friend. It was terrifying and terribly sad for Marc and me to listen to. We were scared to death for Bryan, and there was nothing we could do for him. Despite working with and knowing many people in recovery by this point in my life, this was the first time it was truly "in my house" and the first time I had seen it up close. Until then, I hadn't actually interacted with someone I loved who was high on crystal meth or any other drug, much less trying to come down from it. I had only experienced the *after*—the Shane's and Wasson's of the world who would say, "Oh we've gotten our shit together" and their conversations that revolved around meetings and sponsors and sober parties. This was nothing like that and just one of many occasions in my business life when I would ask the universe, "Where is the adult who is supposed to fix this for me?" I wasn't capable of being the adult to fix this for myself, much less the writhing mess in my guest room.

On the afternoon of his third horrible day with us, Bryan's friends arrived to take him to rehab and that was the last time I saw him for four years. As they drove away, I wondered if I would ever see him again. He seemed so vulnerable; this tough, resolute man that we had nicknamed Macho, no longer lived up to his handle. Surely many business owners have favorite employees they lose touch with at some point, but this felt like an old friend being ripped away.

Fortunately, I did see Bryan again and we have kept in touch over the years. By then he was clean again, for the moment, and I was riding high with four successful stores under my belt. He said something to me then that really resonates with me now. "It's the days in between that count, Gina," he told me. I suddenly realized that Bryan knew he might never be consistently sober, no matter how hard he tried, he might always go back out. But Bryan lived with that because he realized that there would always be the clean periods, *the times in between*, and those were the times that counted.

I realized that during this whole dragged-out struggle to make 5th Street successful, Bryan's battles with addiction were always in the back of my mind. The memory of him was a gentle reminder, along with my sales figures, that everything I did was not always going to be perfect. I was learning, like Bryan had, that sometimes, despite my best efforts, I was destined to fail, but still I needed to keep trying to get to the in-between times. Bryan was thousands of miles away, but his resolve remained an inspiration, his spirit was my hope, and I clung to that. Or at least I tried.

As Bryan tackled his problems head on, I fell back on my typical M.O. I went looking for the next shiny object rather than focusing on the real problem laying at my feet. By the time the store was six years old, we had already moved on to open four new locations. Stores six through 10 had launched and needed attention too, so it took my mind off the brick wall that was 5th Street. They were more successful right out of the gate, and a fun distraction for me because they appeared to be firing on all cylinders. First, we had gone back up to Baltimore. Then, in July of 2010, we dipped our toes into what is technically a suburb of D.C.

In 2012, we opened two locations in the same year. What might have been seen as a manic move for an operation our size just seemed logical with our ambition and opportunities. With this leap, we opened our third location in Baltimore and then tried our hand opening a teeny location—3500 square feet near the National Zoo.

These were all exciting endeavors but couldn't change the fact that 5th Street wasn't pulling its weight. No matter how we ran the numbers there was no clear path, short of some miracle, that would bring the store to profitability. We were faced with two unfortunate choices—file for bankruptcy at that location and face the consequences or trudge along—the little engine that couldn't—until the steam eventually ran out.

Neither Marc nor I could bear filing for bankruptcy. Even using the word in a sentence felt like complete and utter failure. That path could cost us more than time and money for the current operation. We dreaded the future banking issues it could cause down the road when we wanted to open more stores or renovate an existing one.

So, we dug in. While we continued to grow in other markets, Marc continued to battle the greedy landlord and I worked with Rachel, our first ever and very enthusiastic Marketing Manager, to try everything we could think of to make our sales grow.

How to Pick a Landlord

I used to think that I was the candidate being interviewed for a location. Then one of our best landlords, Bruce Levin, told me one day that I need to brag about how great we are and make sure the landlord matched my expectations. He said to cite our customer count, community activity, and how many years we've paid rent on time.

We have also learned to research building owners too.

- Do they have a stake in the community or live far away?
- Do they have a reputation of neighborhood or city participation?
- Do their other tenants have positive things to say about their relationship with the landlord? When a legally binding relationship might last for 10 or more years, it should be a two-way street and work like a good marriage.

There was no tangible sense of community in this blossoming neighborhood, but reading Judy Wicks' memoir *Good Morning Beautiful Business* had inspired me. Judy had held events that became legendary in her urban Philadelphia neighborhood, and I wanted to be just like her. She treated the dining room of her row house restaurant like her living room—serving meals and making memories that carried her successfully through decades of ownership.

With Judy as our muse, Rachel and I schemed up our first annual Ladies Night at 5th Street Ace. We had no idea if women would actually attend, but our plan was to entice our female neighbors with sales, giveaways and an educational girl's night out. My dad never taught me to use power tools, perhaps other women also lacked experience? We would introduce them to their cool retail neighbor (us) and maybe teach them a thing or two in the process. We invited a representative from a power tool company to give demonstrations and asked a couple of local female business owners to join us for the night—giving them an opportunity to mix and mingle with our guests. We hoped that by infusing our local flare we could win over a new contingent of shoppers.

We closed the doors to the public early on a Tuesday and the event started at 6p.m. We had finger foods, soda, and wine—a throwback to the old screwdriver bar days from our first two openings, although by this time I think we were wise enough to get a temporary liquor license. Several of our vendors had donated generous raffle prizes and others had shipped us samples of free stuff to put in 100 gift bags for the first women to walk through the doors.

I stared hard at those cloth bags, lined up in a row and emblazoned with our store name and logo. I could see that dark green color in my sleep, it had become emblematic of my personality. The stores and I had melded as one and it was impossible for me to separate the business from myself and vice versa. In that moment these bags represented my hopes that a failure could be reversed.

That first Ladies' Night was an *in between* time for our store. I heard Bryan's voice telling me to "make it count" and in the long run, it really did, just not in the ways we had hoped it would, or as quickly. The doors were scheduled to open at 6 p.m., and at 5:30 p.m. our first guests started lining up outside for the overflowing gift bags and a chance to hang out with us.

Anticipation among the team started to grow and I found myself straightening vests, giving pep talks over the radio. The minute hand counted down and I yelled "places everyone"—the stage manager preparing her troupe to entertain. This was it! All my hopes and dreams of turning this store around would be made or broken when the doors flung open.

They streamed in in clusters of two or three, a girlfriend brought a couple girlfriends, or a neighbor brought a friend.

Our team had shown up from all over the chain to experience the event firsthand and to help doing the things we do best—giving product advice, running around with a walkie talkie in hand or hosting a mini seminar in some back corner. Oh, and serving drinks. They were enthralled by the throngs of attendees. One of the guys even wore a tuxedo, proud to represent us while demo'ing how to change a light fixture to curious on-lookers.

I watched all of this unfold while wandering the aisles looking for guests to chat up. The feedback was incredible and even though it felt very cramped, we ended the night feeling like a new chapter had indeed begun. Sales weren't great, but we measured our success by the long lines at the two registers, the fact that our vendors distributed all their freebies and that there wasn't a drop of wine left in the joint. Power tools and fermented grapes seemed to have found a place in the hearts of every woman within a four-block radius. We were on to something.

Despite the favorable results though, sad to say, the store did not become a newly reborn overnight success. In fact, I'm not sure we saw any measurable improvement and so we continued to limp along. Ladies' Nights on the other hand, have become a cornerstone of our marketing tactics. Over the years, thousands of women have attended our Ladies' Nights and thousands more have come to other events we've hosted. All proof that some of the discoveries you make while you're failing can lead to new successes down the line. We finally and permanently flipped the "open for business" sign over to closed in 2018 when the lease ran out. Once we cleared out the space, we never looked back. It was bittersweet for me—like the day Bryan was driven away to rehab and I wondered if that was the end.

There were plenty of customers who had opinions on our closing. We had thousands of customers so there were plenty of folks to let down—but not enough to justify our costs and operational pains. I avoided reading the on-line comments—the nice ones made me cry and the bitter ones made me mad. I couldn't win. Instead, I reminded myself repeatedly that I had been warned this could—no, would—happen at some point. At least we had gotten that over with. I also had to admit that we had violated all our own guidelines when we chose the location and overlooked our own rules.

Some business owners might have become soured on expansion after this long dragged-out challenge—much like some of my teammates might become discouraged after a third or fourth bout of rehab. But to me, our resilience reflects the life that Bryan leads—it's abundant and real. We all have to keep trying for those times in between. My in-between times at 5th Street resulted in six more store openings and launching a Ladies' Night tradition that endures to this day.

THIRTEEN

I Bought an Icon

For more than a decade, I harbored a secret dream to own an iconic store on Capitol Hill. To me, Frager's Hardware epitomized success. It was historic, bustling, and nationally known in the hardware world. In short, it was my definition of iconic—the Boardwalk on the Monopoly board of my life.

Started by the Frager family in 1920, Frager's Hardware sits 11 blocks from the majestic United States Capitol. The view down Pennsylvania Avenue is awe-inspiring and even though we have lived in Washington, DC for more than 25 years, Marc never fails to say "Hello Capitol" when we drive over the bridge back into the city after being away. The view from the store, along with the length of its tenure, only adds to the gravitas of being its owner.

The store had stayed in the Frager family for generations until it was purchased in 1975 by two friends, John Weintraub and Ed Copenhaver.[35] When the duo celebrated their 35th anniversary as its owners, I sent them a card that simply said, "When I grow up, I want to be Frager's Hardware." And I meant it. To me, the store represented the pinnacle of brick-and-mortar fame, something I could aspire to with my own growing team. Apparently, my outreach stuck with John and although I couldn't have known it then, I had inked our future in that single handwritten fan letter.

I may have also written the foreshadowing of joining a long-fought debate that rages among my peer group about what's easier—opening a brand-new store from scratch or buying an existing location with all the history, both good and bad, that comes along with it.

This argument only gets louder when the subject at hand has become a legend in its industry. Are iconic businesses made or do they happen organically? Are they a happy accident after decades of operation, or are they created on purpose? If one buys an icon, does it remain so automatically? Does it pose added responsibility for the new owners, and could I ever live up to that challenge?

I've always had an enthusiastic infatuation with locally built icons like Zingerman's, Powell's Books, and Ben's Chili Bowl. There are small powerhouses dotted throughout the country that are famous in one form or another. Marc and friends were quick to point out that one doesn't need to be "local" to be an icon and that I should include such worldwide brands like McDonald's, Starbucks, and Ford on my list.

When asked about building such a brand, a few of my store managers sent me answers that were both thoughtful and thought provoking. Jackie responded that three key attributes needed to be in place: uniqueness, consistency, and exceptional customer service. Interestingly, she went on to say that "longevity does not equal iconic."

A second manager, Aileng, was quick to disagree, however, and said, "To be an icon takes time." Frager's, for example, has had a hundred years to do so and it is well-deserved. Aileng went on to say, "Gina, we can grow an iconic business on purpose."

Francis's opinion was even more nuanced. He thinks nothing grows to become iconic unless it's built in an iconic neighborhood—places like the French Quarter, South Beach or Hollywood where people are proud to live in nationally famous neighborhoods and wear that pride on t-shirts or bumper stickers. Like supporting the hometown football team regardless of town size—all it takes is a vibrant spirit and maybe a silkscreen machine for iconography to grow.

Of the 14 locations we have owned over the years, we have built 10 and purchased four. All but one of them is way too young to be put in a category called icon if you agree that they do only evolve over time. Each opportunity brought a unique set of challenges and overcoming one obstacle always seemed to give rise to three new ones.

A wise teammate once comically asked, "Do you just keep opening more locations so we can fix our screw ups from the last one?"

I must admit I do have a perverse sense of "Just give me one more shot to do this right" when it comes to new spots.

I'm still not sure where I side on the subject of "buy versus build," but I could absolutely write an entire book on the pros and cons of each method of expansion. In fact, it might need to be a trilogy to document the pitfalls and joys we experienced when Frager's became ours. After all, what changes can you make to improve upon something that was never broken in the eyes of adoring generations of shoppers? Frager's is more than just a store, it's unquestionably an icon, whatever that entails. Frager's was *it*.

After building 10 locations from scratch, I had never faced this dilemma. When Old Town Ace became one of our many, we truly bought a mess. It had less than half the required inventory, a manager that was stealing products out the back door, and a customer base that had lowered every ounce of its community's expectations. For us, there was no way but up and Old Town Ace thrived under our ownership. We renovated, restocked, reenergized, and hired a fantastic manager who entrenched himself in that store in the exact ways it needed. Wouldn't they all be this easy? Sure, the transition required some serious elbow grease, but grease was part of our DNA. And our product line.

Our mettle was really put to the test in 2017 with Frager's.

In addition to being almost a century old, years prior to our deal-making, Frager's had suffered a terrible fire that hadn't just threatened to put an end to the whole operation but had solidified Frager's place in the Capitol Hill community as a legend to protect.

An errant cigarette butt, thrown into a garbage can behind the store, reduced the building to a pile of ash in a matter of hours.

Charred bricks and a scorched portion of the original sign were all that remained of the nonagenarian landmark on Pennsylvania Ave. I was across town on the day of its demise, and from three miles away, I could see the incredible plumes of smoke and hear the screams of the sirens racing to the scene. It felt as if the entire city might be burning and my phone began to blow up. Friends and customers were calling to make sure it wasn't one of my locations and I remember feeling incredibly grateful that it wasn't. At least not yet.

Before the smoke even cleared, the generous Capitol Hill community rallied in a way that rivaled an old-fashioned barn raising. Tens of thousands of dollars were donated to a fund to ensure the staff could keep being paid. The DC government provided a temporary location for the store to operate in the interim, and there was a makeshift Frager's up and running in less than a week. To me, this seemed like a further affirmation of the community spirit and support we would be buying into.

It wasn't long before the fire was a thing of the past for the team and customers. John Weintraub, however, had a mountain of work to do between insurance agencies, construction companies and a whole host of other entities. The longer these battles ensued, the closer he got to throwing in the towel.

Two years after the fire, I got a call that would change my life. The day that John called to ask if we would buy his store was like a day filled with fireworks—everything seemed brighter and more electrifying in our world once Frager's entered the picture. I was so excited that my dream was going to become a reality and my enthusiasm rivalled that of when I had signed that first lease for Logan Hardware more than a decade before. Finally, Boardwalk would be mine.

John, Marc and I made a handshake deal that then took two years to play out—there were valuations to be done, mounds of paperwork to sign and lawyers had to get involved. All the while we negotiated and waited, I was building an intricate fantasy in my imagination of how incredibly smooth and positive the transition would be once we finally assumed ownership.

These types of negotiations normally occur in a shroud of secrecy. No one wants word to leak out lest the deal fall apart. A presale uprising or too much press can stall or stop the entire production, so Marc and I could only keep the negotiations to ourselves and scheme between the two of us. We kept everyone else in the dark until at long last, the paperwork was complete.

I might be able to chuckle about it now, but let's just say taking over our newest addition was not as seamless as it had been in my fantasy. As it turned out, nobody seemed happy that we purchased the store. The Frager's team wasn't happy, the community wasn't happy and my oversized desire to be liked and embraced by the neighbors went right out the window. An early review admonished, "Frager's was once a wonderful community asset with a long history and an experienced, knowledgeable and caring staff. That was no more after A Few Cool Hardware stores took over. In a stroke, they lost a base of institutional knowledge which had taken decades to assemble."

We hosted a big retirement party in the garden center for John after the sale went through and more than 200 neighbors RSVP'd to attend. I teased him that they only came to make sure I didn't have two heads. John was 74 that year and I believed he had a well-earned retirement coming. He deserved to live out his golden years with his wife Fran after decades of taking care of the Frager's team and the community. The community, however, wasn't ready to let go of "their person." To them, John was the store—he was what made it theirs and right and whole. Regardless of it being in a temporary location and him being exhausted, many could not get past the store changing hands.

I was asked repeatedly where I was from, why I was qualified to buy the store and if I was going to change anything. Later I would learn that "change anything" also included some creaky old floors that had been burned when the building had. As we stood amongst the well-wishers that day, I began to finally grasp the scope of the challenge ahead of me.

I have read countless examples over the years of this kind of reputation getting in the way of and indeed ruining, the transition of a long-standing, often multi-generational business. Owners who could not get past not being there, simply eliminated *the there*. They shut down the business and walked away, unable or unwilling to find a buyer to carry on the legacy. I feared that if we didn't buy Frager's from John, all the years he spent building this legend could simply be erased, reduced to a pile of ash just like the location burned in the fire. There were some hurtful emails from folks telling me they were taking their business elsewhere. One customer named Paul wrote, "It used to mean a huge and wonderful hardware store. Now it is a brand name under Ace—nowhere near as good as the original."

Notes like these accentuated the misunderstanding that

surrounds cooperatives, not to mention that we had added about 4,000 square feet to the size of the store. Customers didn't understand that Ace was not a national chain swooping in on their beloved store. In fact, Frager's had previously been a part of the True Value Co-op, which, operationally, was almost identical. I took all the negativity personally and found myself avoiding phone calls or voicemail in case I had to hear another complaint. To be honest, I could have handled emotions that leaned sad or nostalgic. But most of the calls or emails I received were downright rude. My assistant, trying to cheer me up one day said, "Well, just think of the calls the CEO of Home Depot gets."

I tried to remind myself that this purchase wasn't about me or my team or even the business we were building. It was about ensuring that a community could keep its hardware store. I know now that because I had an idealized picture of Frager's, I was JUST like the community. I had such reverence that I went in with my eyes wide shut—no regard for the struggle this change was going to cause everyone or how emotionally complex it would be for me. Hadn't I learned from Wasson all those years ago that change is really fricking hard?

It wasn't long after the purchase that I was reminded of a lesson I learned years ago from a teammate named Eric. Dedicated to building his best life, he once said to me, "Gina, it's better to be respected than liked."

Eric had worked in our first location for about a year when I decided to ask him to step up into an assistant manager's role. I was so proud of him and impressed by his work ethic. He was diligent, respected, and punctual. I assumed he was eager to grow his influence and paycheck because, well, isn't everyone?

One day I took him to a local coffee shop for a chat. I wanted to talk to him about his future, and whether he felt ready for more responsibility.

Eric interrupted me mid-sentence. "Nope," he said stubbornly, before I even had a chance to ask the entire question. "I do not want a promotion and you can't bully me into it."

Eric is statuesque. He stands very erect and has hands the size of Texas. I have no doubt it looked comical to see his six-foot six frame towering over me at five foot two, calling me a bully.

Eric's issue was a horrible lack of self-confidence stemming from years of drug abuse. This experience was still too early in our growth for me to have fully grasped the havoc drugs can wreak on one's psyche. It had never occurred to me that I would face this manner of resistance, especially to what I perceived as an incredibly positive occasion. What Eric craved was stability. Comfort. Sameness. What he found in his daily routine at Logan Hardware allowed him to learn and continue to heal surrounded by teammates who appreciated his consistency as a retail associate.

My Hero, Terry Flood

Sometime around 2007, I got a call from a woman named Terry who was the Executive Director of a program called Jubilee Jobs whose motto is Dignity, Sustenance and Hope. Terry and her small team worked to place DC residents in jobs around the city. Many of their applicants had been out of the work force for a variety of reasons such as addiction or incarceration and were often seen as unemployable. I had been unknowingly hiring applicants from Jubilee Jobs for several years, a testament I think to Jubilee's job preparation courses, and we became one of their model employers. I eventually joined their corporate advisory board, which I think ultimately launched my advocacy work in a bigger way. Incidentally, Eric was a Jubilee Jobs applicant.

Eric and I did the same dance twice in a six-month period and both times he firmly shot me down. Then one day, on his own terms and with a big grin on his face, Eric told me he was finally ready to accept my offer to promote him. He would take on the added responsibility, learn to manage a team, and receive a bigger paycheck.

Marc has been known to call me the hurricane, because I whip my life and everything adjacent into a frenzy of motion and it's true, I am driven and my enthusiasm for any kind of project often gets the best of me. Eric moved through life differently than I did. He taught me that it's okay to do things on your own terms, at a pace you are comfortable with, and his pace was methodical, and at times, glacial.

He was eventually tapped to lead our brand-new location in Takoma Park where he filled the management role for eight years. I don't think there was a resident there who didn't know or love him. He was the grand marshal of the 4th of July parade, wore fun pajamas for the annual community pajama-jam sale, and maintained the cleanest store in our chain. I liked to joke that if he quit, we would have to close the store because the customers would never let me live it down. His team also respected the hell out of him.

Eric's advice rang true in so many ways. We had to do the right thing by our customers, operate with integrity, provide value and quality, and eventually the community would respond with their support and respect. It didn't matter if the team or customers liked me—this wasn't a popularity contest, it was business. My desire to always win might only be outshined by my desire to be liked. By everyone. I can hear a lecture from Eric every time I think of this story. My contrasting personality traits do battle for World Conqueror and Miss Congeniality at the same time and one of them must always be crowned.

I can't say I stopped taking negative comments personally, but I did focus on integrating the store into our large family of stores and tried to stop being star struck by my own storefront. We had inventory to clean up, a software system to merge, and over 40 new employees to teach our way of retailing.

We had lots to learn from Frager's too. They hadn't made it this long by doing all the wrong things. They had just done many of them differently than us and we had to fuse operations in a way that allowed us all to move forward.

Professor and researcher Vicki TenHaken cites the Japanese word *shinise*, for businesses that have been around for at least 100 years.[36] She says these businesses would not have lasted so long if they hadn't found a way to "change and improve." It's the delicate balance of "tradition and change" that will carry a business into its next century.

For us, reinventing Frager's was about doing the right things to ensure that a hardware store that I had admired and that had served the same neighborhood for 100 years was given a chance to keep going—to rise from the ashes (literally) in a new way, with new owners. The most I could expect from the community is that they kept shopping there—supporting us in the only way we would stay in business. It might take a while for the community to like us, but hopefully, once they saw us upholding our values and maintaining consistency and quality, perhaps they would even grow to love us.

FOURTEEN

There's a Dragon in My Living Room

One day, a bearded dragon named Gabe who eats live crickets and meal worms came to live with me. He was an okay house guest for the most part. He didn't really do much except hide in his little cave or spend hours lounging on top of it to get closer to the heat lamp above his head—scales stretched taut, a look of pure contentment on his face. Gabe's eye lids are a pretty shade of blue which belies his reptilian masculinity. A friend hysterically called him "the perfect stoner pet." He seems blissfully unaware of what is going on around him including that my dog, Buckley, walks by his cage each morning and gives him the stink eye.

One day, Gabe and the dog seemed to figure out simultaneously that they were co-existing in the same house, and I was witness to the whole comical exchange. Bearded dragons' necks puff out when they are alarmed, and Gabe's grew exponentially as he whipped his head toward the glass when he saw Buckley strutting by. The dog did a double take and he stopped dead in his tracks, eyes bugged out at the glass structure. Gabe was frozen, not a single muscle twitched in his leathery body.

The whole exchange lasted less than a minute but for me it represented *realization*—the recognition that not everyone is the same, that perfect little worlds can be shattered, or perhaps that we can all wake up with a need to change our perspective on the world in order to acknowledge that things we never dreamed of really do exist. Such was the case with Mary who was the reason Gabe was cohabiting with Marc, Buckley and me in the first place. It may surprise you, but I don't walk around the office saying, "Hey, tell me about something shitty from your past!" But throughout the years and without knowing it, we have hired people on welfare, several (actively) homeless men, women battling domestic violence issues, people suffering from mental health issues—people with so many experiences that I am incredibly grateful never to have lived through myself.

Marcus came to work with us when he was still living as a woman. Her name was Mary then and she had grown up a foster kid who had aged out of the system a few years prior. She was also a house plant whisperer. I knew millennials had reignited a passion for indoor greenery but prejudicially, a young Black woman with dreadlocks did not fit my stereotype of a plant-loving millennial for some stupid reason.

Mary was hired at our smallest D.C. location near the National Zoo, and she quickly proceeded to get herself fired for being late *all the time*. We have, by most standards, a lenient tardiness policy and you have to work really hard to be terminated for being late, but she had managed it. If we have learned anything over the years, it is that there needs to be accountability or the whole team can fall apart, so we had to let her go. I am probably the worst at enforcing this lesson, but I swear I understand why it's important and I will keep trying.

Here's the rub though, Mary LOVED her job. She was so sad when she got fired that as soon as she signed her termination letter, she asked for her job back. Tenacity. We like that.

Our Director of HR told Mary that she should go get her old grocery store job back, continue to learn and mature, and that maybe, just maybe, we would hire her back if we had an opening at some point in the future.

Every two weeks, the call happened like this:

"Hello Ann Marie, it's me again, Mary. Can I have my old job back?"

"Sorry Mary, we don't have a position for you right now."

"Oh, okay, then..."

Click.

This dialing dance happened for about 10 weeks until Ann Marie finally relented. That day, I overheard her say, "Mary, I'm tired of answering your calls. Give your current boss two weeks' notice then report to Logan Hardware after you're all squared away."

After Mary returned to her happy place, she liked to boast that she was never late again. When she showed up one day with green hair to match the plants she had fallen in love with, you know what? No one thought it was odd. She knew she was home, and so did we.

Two-and-a-half years after Mary came back and a few short months before Gabe the lizard became my new roomie, Mary told her manager she wanted to become Marcus. She needed to leave Mary behind and become the man she had always known she was meant to be. Speaking his truth didn't yet come naturally. The stress swam in his head and was apparent in his eyes.

Tim, our manager, looked right at him and said, "Marcus, it's not for people to *understand*, it's for them to *accept*." It wasn't long after this exchange that Marcus's life began to unravel. Sometime in the middle of 2020, I became aware of some trouble between Marcus and his leadership team. Marcus is pretty good at expressing his feelings and if he is depressed, he'll either let us know, or he just won't show up. I began to witness an internal struggle that was so visible, so apparent at least to me that it was like watching a game of tug-o-war.

Marcus had been given more leadership responsibility by then. He managed shifts, had keys to the store, and was responsible for keeping the workday flowing. I was starting to believe I was watching a future store manager blossom before my eyes. But whether it was the pressure of his new duties, the pressures of his transition or his history catching up to him, Marcus was slowly succumbing to alcoholism. He would call off shifts with mysterious illnesses and used depression as an excuse for what may well have been hangover-induced shame. He began neglecting his appearance and his professionalism suffered. His hair, dyed a vibrant green, dulled, along with his smile, and the cheerful employee who stopped by my office every day to say hello began to avoid me.

Contradictorily, if there was written communication needed between a store leader and a customer, the email exchanges between Marcus and our guests could not have been better articulated. I would read these exchanges in awe—if even half the team could communicate as well as he did, we would be on top of the world—I so desperately wanted to believe that each one of these bits of prose meant that some improvement was happening—that Marcus was *figuring it all out* and that we wouldn't have to take some kind of action to correct the course. This would not be the first time we had watched a teammate succumb to an addiction, but each time I secretly hoped it would somehow miraculously just go away.

Real adults show up in these situations and there have been times when I've selfishly prayed for that real adult to show up and save *me* from having to be that grownup. But you know what, that is the same brand of denial and the avoidance that puts young people like Marcus on their path in the first place. Not the going from Mary to Marcus part, because that's wonderful. But a history of neglect that had failed to prepare him for life, and a tendency to use evasiveness to avoid confronting his problems.

Gradually, we realized we were watching Marcus' life fall apart. He needed an intervention. Later, when we had time to reflect on what we had watched unfold, it was as if alcohol had jettisoned Marcus headfirst into the life he wanted but could not freely access on his own. Two of our core values: "Always Grow and Share" and "Embrace and Drive Change" collided and then merged in Marcus's life. In order to *grow*, he needed to *change* in a really big way and that drove him to the brink. Our values didn't need to shape his work life. They needed to be embodied in his *life* life.

A mutual friend, who I mistakenly assumed had participated in past interventions, asked me to help her with the conversation. It turns out she needed the fortitude and support that my presence would bring, so it was co-dependency to the rescue.

Lines from a poem Marcus had shared gave us a glimpse of a lifetime of struggle and perhaps his perceived benefit—or relief from—self-medicating his way through life.

Should I pretend like everything is okay? People are fast to tell me what I need to do but take a minute and hop in my shoes.

Neglected, abused since age two

Dumped and taken by the government, age 5

Beat and molested til age 15

Lost and confused til 18

Strung out dependent on drugs, alcohol, tobacco from 16 til now

Depressed Depressed Depressed

How in the hell can I even focus on just one thing when I'm in an everlasting battle with myself. Thanking God for the people who helped, the people who actually cared. The people who gave without an opened hand.

Give me shelter. Give me a chance to be all I can be. Just give me a chance to be me.

There are over 420,000 foster kids nationwide[37] and around 20,000 age out of the system annually.[38] Many of these young adults have no other support system e.g., relatives, teachers, mentors, or even jobs with a nurturing leader so they often fall through the cracks. Within four years of aging out, 70% will be on government assistance,[39] 25% will not have completed high school and only around 4% will earn a college degree.[40]

One 2011 study found that less than 50% of young adults who have aged out of foster care will have no earnings and those who do, earn on average only $7500 per year by the age of 26.[41] A lack of skills and resources keeps this group of young people on the fringe for life. It appeared that this was beginning to happen to Marcus.

This is how Natasha and I found ourselves on a Zoom call with Marcus, our fingers crossed, hoping to encourage him to quietly head to treatment. A local, and incredibly bucolic facility with a reputation for success had offered him a scholarship. This was a gift of $30,000 a month for free and an opportunity to heal. This was a way forward from an abusive past and a self-destructive present. There was no way we could let Marcus turn down this opportunity.

Skippy was on my mind the entire day leading up to the call. If I'm being honest, I don't think I had been in a place to help him all those years ago when he needed it most. I had been treading water as a young business owner, overlooking the hard stuff unless it was my hard stuff. I wasn't going to let that happen this time around, I was out for redemption.

The call started out okay. We didn't beat around the bush and Marcus was smart enough to figure out what was up. We had never all been on a call like this before and there was no reason for us to be, unless the reason was him. Eventually the tears started to flow. Natasha and I both later admitted that we had been holding back our own, playing the adults and powering through. I wanted to reach through the screen and give Marcus a hug—an enveloping embrace that I always think solves a problem.

"What about my bills?" he asked. Marcus's shoulders slouched; his face tensed up.

"I'll pay them," I said, without even thinking about it. It was after all, the only logical response. I took a deep breath. *I've got this.*

"What about my job?" Marcus said, lifting his eyebrows a bit. He was sure that the woman who provides jobs wouldn't be able to make him leave his.

"We'll save it for when you come back," I said. Now I was in true boss mode, I had the power to ensure that this was true.

Marcus paused, gulped a big breath of air and pushed out his last-ditch effort at evading the inevitable.

"Well, what about Gabe?" he asked in a small, barely audible voice.

Marcus's personal excuses to avoid going to rehab unfolded in what he considered levels of severity—how could he drop out of life with the grown-up responsibilities of bills and work, and a pet?

When I related this story weeks later to my friend Brian he said, "You know Gina, no other employer would do all this." But I don't like to lose, and this was a game I was willing to go all in for.

"I'll take the dragon," I said. *How hard could it be?* I thought, naively.

Marcus's shoulders slumped and his face relaxed. His body language demonstrated that he was out of excuses. I had foiled every one of them. I was reminded of a quote that Marcus wrote on his Facebook page one day—"Sometimes you think that you want to disappear, but all you really want is to be found." Here was his chance to really be *seen*, supported, and to really get better.

And that's what happened. Marcus went off to get better, and I became the proud foster momma of an overgrown lizard.

I don't know what Marcus' future holds—I do know that he has all the potential in the world. I watched him grow and change beyond his life in our hardware store and I had to be okay with that and let him go. Maybe being a good leader also means embracing employee development in ways that move them beyond your reach.

Marcus is living a sober life now—he has a nice home and is learning how to live one day at a time. He sent me a text message recently that read, "Thank you for not giving up on me because I wouldn't have made it to today if I'd been anywhere else. Thank you for being a kind and caring human and thank you for teaching me so much."

The words made my heart swell and all I could think was: *Really? It was he who taught me.*

Oh! Gabe is living his best life too. He has a bigger cage, a new dragon friend to hang out with and a dad who is now healthy enough to love them both.

Life Lessons from a Dragon

For someone as extroverted as I am, there is a lot to learn from a bearded dragon. I'm not saying I'd ever want one of my own, but I did take away a few lessons from my time with Gabe.

- Manage your body temperature. Dragons worship the heat lamp and since I'm always cold or hot, I learned to pay more attention to how my surroundings affect how I'm working.
- Eat sparingly. While I didn't enjoy watching crickets being hunted, Gabe only ate when necessary and never overindulged. If he only wanted two of 10 crickets, he only ate two of them.
- Don't use up energy unnecessarily. The perfect reminder for those of us who run a little hyper.

FIFTEEN

Our Pride Is Serving You

I f freedom, love, and frivolity all had a baby, it would be a gay pride parade. For most of the people in our neighborhood, the DC Pride parade is cause for a giant celebration—a day that started as an act of defiance has become a joyous festival of inclusion and equality. For those of us fortunate enough to be located along the parade route, the event is completely immersive. Houses and businesses unfurl banners and flags out of windows, sidewalks are decorated with chalk murals and tiny row house yards are filled with signs, sparkly lights and makeshift bleachers to host the day-long party about to burst out of doors.

My favorite row house in the neighborhood has a riotous display of Barbie dolls arranged in a vignette in their front yard. The outfits and décor change based on the season. For Pride, the Barbies are all decked out in a rainbow of colors. The Barbies are often the subject of local blogs or Facebook posts and never fail to cause one to pause and smile. Occasionally, someone who obviously isn't from Logan Circle posts something about being offended by the *scantily clad dolls* on Q Street, but no one cares what they think anyway.

Pride is celebrated for the entire month of June in Washington, DC, but the grand finale revolves around the parade and the Pride festival that takes place downtown. This huge party with music and dancing that lasts all day is within eyesight of the White House, and I can only imagine it started as an F-U to some unsupportive administration in the 1980s.

Summer in Washington can be brutal—while the humidity threatens to do us all in, the parts of the city that are more concrete than trees and can be slightly unbearable. Rainstorms are the norm. But the weather always seems to bless parade day and revelers are more likely to be sunburned and happy than drenched. It's as if the skies know it is a day for merriment and celebration and vow to do their part.

In 2014, after spending 11 years in the original Logan Hardware space on P Street, our lease had run out. We have learned over the years to negotiate extension terms but when we signed our first lease in 2002, we weren't savvy enough to do that. With no extensions to re-up and a landlord no longer willing to negotiate what he once considered a feather in his cap, the time had come for us to move on and into a less restrictive space four blocks north.

We would be taking over newly renovated digs twice the size, with an honest-to-goodness elevator and actual professional office space. Despite knowing it was a great move for us, I was tremendously sad. Like a first-born child heading off to college or moving out of a beloved home and wondering if you'll ever have the perfect reading nook again, I was sad for what I thought I would miss. One of my favorite words in the Portuguese language is *saudade*, which translates basically as *longing*. I felt saudade for the old space before we had even handed the keys back. I knew the move was good for us, like exchanging a tricycle for the big-girl two-wheeler. For goodness' sake, it was only a quarter of a mile away, but it felt like a Really Big Deal.

I didn't visit the store once while the products were being packed away, unable and unwilling to face the dismantling of the shelves and the reliving of the months it had taken to put them together. If it counts as a superpower, my ability to compartmentalize and avoid situations that could hurt my heart is one of mine. I couldn't stand on the creaky old wooden floorboards and think about how I would never do that again. There were so many things wrong with that space but in my heart, it was *the one*. I wondered if Ray Kroc or Howard Schultz ever felt this way about the first McDonalds or the first Starbucks. Everything that followed from 2003 on had flowed from that original space.

However, eventually, the day came when I had to pay witness to the end. Someone on my team called. "Come see the progress!" he said. "You're going to be really impressed." "Okay," I said. I couldn't think of a real reason to say no. Later that day I steeled myself to walk through the door—I could see from the large storefront window that I wasn't going to like what I walked into, and my feet felt stuck to the sidewalk. It was if all the gum that dotted it had jumped up underneath every inch of my sneakers. The old glass door finally flung open. A teammate beaming and proud of his accomplishments, oblivious to my feelings, came bounding out to invite me in.

The question *What if?* kept repeating itself in my head. *What if I hadn't moved to Logan Circle?* There are times when this question has made me panic thinking that Marc and I might have never gotten married. *What if I hadn't dreamed of opening a hardware store?* Odd that my mind never returned to my failed attempts at a tech career. *What if the landlord hadn't let me lease this first space?* And worst of all, *what if Richard hadn't lied to me about Ace's approval?* That last one chokes me up even today. So much of what we have accomplished over the last 11 years has come from hope or dreams or even walking blindfolded. And some of it has even flowed from deceit. Thank goodness.

So, I held my breath and got ready to walk through those doors one final time. It sounds so dramatic now—it was just a crumbly old building—but to me it represented hopes and goals and sweat and tears. And the tears flowed again the second I crossed the threshold. I am never ashamed to show vulnerability in front of my teammates. I choose to think it humanizes "the boss," and they can go work for an asshole if an expression of genuine emotion makes them uncomfortable.

There were big smiles on the team's faces that day. Thousands (and thousands) of pounds of steel shelving had been carried down the narrow stairwell and out onto the bed of a truck. What was left looked sad and forgotten, like things even the dumpster wouldn't want. Everyone was so proud of themselves and wanted the pat on the back that I was sure to give them now that I had come by. I dried my soggy eyes and jumped up and down at the progress. I plastered a smile on my face and let myself be led through each nearly bare section.

It was truly remarkable to see it all again, almost naked and empty. Every so often there was a signature on the wall, an autograph of the friend who had constructed the shelving that stood there. Smiley faces or names or a simple doodle brought me back to the months and months it had taken to set the place up. Friends or co-workers from Marc's tech job would arrive on a Saturday and spend a few hours doing manual labor with us. It was a welcome change from their desk jobs, and we were all young enough to think it was good fun.

I was so consumed with *everything* when we were originally setting the space up that nothing had stood out. Standing here today I could re-see the possibilities that had first drawn me to the space. It was the right space at the right time. And now, it was the right time to move on.

However, we weren't going to do that without as much fanfare as we could rally! We were a community gathering place, a place where diversity was celebrated, where freedom of expression flourished, and we knew just the way to go out with a bang.

Logan Hardware had always been on the Pride parade route and teammates would set up a party tent on the sidewalk where we handed out water or beads while selling various items of rainbow hued paraphernalia to parade goers and passersby.

Parade day is embraced by our entire team—employees from our other locations come by just to hang out for the day, pitch in when needed, and dance on the sidewalk with us. It is a unifying day with lines between gay and straight, boss and employee, customer and cashier all erased. It is also impossible not to bubble over with joy.

The year we moved, my assistant, Todd Lumpkin, decided on his own and then convinced us that we wouldn't just be ON the route that year, we would also be IN the parade. "The hardware crew," he said, "has to be an integral part of that passing bit of joy to celebrate the fact that we are moving to a new spot in the neighborhood."

The feeling we wanted to evoke was like taking a best friend by the hand and leading them on a new road home.

Despite having all the tools we could need at our disposal, we didn't have a lot of time to build a masterpiece float. We did however have an absurd amount of enthusiasm and what Marc likes to call "working man strength" from running around the store all day. So, we painted some pallets with the name of the store, added wheels and planned to push the "float" for the several miles of the parade route while decked out in our custom-made t-shirts. We invited teammates from all our stores and even had some folks from Baltimore come down to join us. A few customers, lured in by the fun, donned costumes and threw themselves into the mix.

At this point in my life, my favorite mode of transportation was an adult tricycle I had named Billy after a childhood friend. Our friends Fred and Christine came to "float" with us that day, and with flasks of vodka hidden under their funny costumes they took turns riding Billy along the entire route while the rest of us walked.

Leading up to parade day, Todd kept dropping hints about the costumes Marc and I would wear. He wasn't going to tell us—no amount of bribing or "bossing" could drag it out of him. I actually think he made other staff members sign non-disclosure agreements because he really couldn't keep a secret and had to tell *someone*. All I know is that when the subject came up, everyone around us would start giggling and try to walk away before spilling the beans. Our only instructions were to "dress lightly and wear comfortable shoes."

We arrived at our designated meeting spot in Dupont Circle about three hours prior to the kickoff. It's a well-known fact that damn near everyone in the parade will usually have spent the previous night partying and will inevitably show up very late and famously hungover. The organizers are smart to put in some cushion time. Our ragtag crew was a punctual one—not to mention that half were in recovery, so the previous night had been spent in meetings, not in a bottle. We were ready to go!

The costumes finally came out of their bags, Todd presented them with an exaggerated display of fanfare, very clearly proud of himself. Mine was in the shape of a saw—I would be dressed head to toe in felt with jagged edges. I had worn red lipstick that day, so the result was some sort of comic book home improvement tool, I guess. The more Christine drank from her flask, the more she yelled, "I looooooove the red lip, Gina!" as if I had only one.

Marc won the day, though—hell, he kind of won the entire parade. He was dressed up as a human drill—as in a power tool with the bit coming straight out from you-know-where. He couldn't have been funnier dancing through the streets, and every reveler wanted their photo taken with the slightly naughty get up. It was brilliant and Todd was over-the-moon proud.

It was also further proof that I had married the best man in the world—not an ounce of shame in his body and more than happy to perform for and take cheers from the thousands of gay men along the route who appreciated the get-up.

The entire production took about three hours once we finally launched, and we must have burned 10,000 calories dancing our way from the beginning of the route to where we finally ended in the middle of 14th Street. The pallets on wheels might have been a good idea on the drawing board but they were hard to push up even a slightly sloping road for a long period of time. All we could do was laugh and take turns with everyone on the team demonstrating the patience they used to provide great customer service.

We were continuously buoyed along by the many familiar faces in the waving crowds on the side of the road. Everyone goes to the parade, so we were cheered on by children we knew from store visits, couples with their dogs, parents who had come to support their LGBTQ+ children, and the whole cast of characters who had made the last 11 years a success for us. It was one of the most fun and fulfilling days of our lives.

I learned that day once more that it's not the four physical walls that had propped us up for over a decade that made our store a success. Nor was it a physical space that would carry us for years to come. It's the community—the ones we build and the ones that surround us and the ones that work with us. We have built a transportable business out of a business that builds things. The residents of Logan Circle supported us from the beginning and the parade was our way of grabbing them all by the hand

and bringing them along to our new place, the next iteration of Logan Hardware just a few blocks away in a brand-new, unconventional home. And while I still felt a bit wistful about leaving the old flagship, I also understood that the heart and soul of Logan Hardware was marching right along with us, to our next stop along the road.

My Inspiration, Small Giants

It's hard not to find inspiration from other great business owners around the country. In 2010, I read a book called *Small Giants* by Bo Burlingham. First published in 2005, the author set out to spotlight business owners and entrepreneurs around the United States who got "big" by staying small. Each company he wrote about was a powerhouse in some way yet maintained a small footprint. Think about it, large stock driven companies are required, or even forced to grow and build more and more wealth every single year.

Zingerman's Delicatessen was founded in 1982 by Ari Weinzweig and Paul Saginaw in Ann Arbor, Michigan. The sandwich shop became so well known that people from all over the country beg them to franchise so they could have Zingerman's in California or Ohio or Colorado.

The guys were steadfast, though, and while they had aspirations for growth, they agreed never to go outside of the boundaries of Washtenaw County where their deli was located. In order to stay true to this plan AND still continue to grow, they had to really think creatively. Today, Zingerman's Community of Businesses is comprised of 10 businesses that all complement each other in one way or another such as the Zingerman's bakery that supplies the deli with bread or the Zingerman's creamery that supplies the Zingerman's coffee shop with its dairy products. Small and mighty.

I've learned many lessons from this book and reference it often when I feel like I'm stuck in a "hardware rut."

SIXTEEN

The Beginning, Not the End

"Every new Beginning comes from some other beginning's
end."
—"Closing Time," Semisonic (1998)

No one magically knows what will happen when they start
a business. When I stop and try really hard to remember
how I felt when I flipped over the OPEN sign on Logan
Hardware almost two decades ago, I struggle to remember
the challenges—to truly re-live the stress and worries and
uncertainties that I must have felt then.

Instead, my mind immediately settles on the people, the warm
memories or the sometimes hurtful or sad stories that flood
back in to fill my head and heart. Business is about people, and

I have been privileged to work with some incredibly resilient, thoughtful, and hardworking people over the years. Who knows if I ever expected to employ 300 people in several cities, I honestly don't remember having that vision early on?

So often I am reminded that a great deal of what I have learned has come from an unlikely place—an addict opening up, sharing with me, teaching me. We grew together over the years and my trajectory would not have been as impactful had it not been for the legions of drug users who deserve to be known by something other than an addiction that became a defining point of their lives.

The beauty of memoir is hindsight—and for me, that hindsight is overwhelmingly positive. Marc is quick to remind me that you must have a bad day to appreciate a good one, so I must admit that as a business owner, I've had my share of those too. If I could wish one thing for anyone starting a business, or anyone really, it is that the good days far outweigh the bad ones, and that you are able to dwell on the plus sides.

The *what if's* loom large for me—what if I hadn't adopted a big dopey dog or handed the leash off to Tommy? What if Shane, John, or Skippy hadn't walked through my door and asked me to join the team? What if Bryan hadn't stayed clean enough to live some *in-between* time in a little store that sold nuts and bolts?

For these guys, and countless others, the store became their lives, as it did ours, and the ties that intertwine us together will last forever. Most people think of an exit strategy as The End as opposed to a new beginning for the business. Even the phrase *exit strategy* evokes a sense of *sayonara* or *see ya, wouldn't wanna be ya*. When I opened Logan Hardware in 2003, I hadn't counted on becoming so attached to my team, but eventually I started worrying about their future.

If we believe that businesses go through the cycle of life, much like human beings, then I want mine to be on an infinity loop. As the founder, this is my baby, the business I dreamed about under that dryer in my mom's salon, and the dream that I grew, built and fought for. Imagining it going away is unfathomable.

This is how I found myself standing at the head of a conference room staring out at 38 of my teammates on August 3, 2021, ready to announce the next part of the journey, and how I intended to continue the loop. My hands were shaking uncharacteristically, my heart beating at 100 miles an hour. I had jotted some notes down but had so many things I wanted to remember to say I was sure I would forget something. My head and my heart were full. We were about to make the announcement that had been years in the making.

When I started to speak, the room got very quiet and I willed my eyes not to immediately well up. Directly in front of me was Mark Wasson. Near him was the always supportive Dave Evans, Manager of our Federal Hill location and our first hire when we made our foray into Baltimore. Around the room were faces that have come to mean so much to me—like old friends who had stopped by for a long overdue lunch.

To my left sat Marc, my husband, best friend, and scheming partner in what I was about to announce. He might like to say there are no tears in hardware but on that day, there would be plenty from both of us. I wanted to jump up and down and bawl at the same time.

"I am sure you all wonder why we are here and what we have planned," I began. Then I asked them to indulge me a trip down memory lane, which led me to the ultimate announcement—that we had formed an Employee Stock Ownership Plan (ESOP) and the people in the room were no longer just my teammates, they were now our partners.

In that moment, 160 of my teammates became co-owners in the company and many others would join them over time. My hope is that everyone on the team, all the future cashiers, sales associates, key makers and delivery drivers will pause when they're helping a customer and think: *What would an owner do?* And they will know, because they'll remember: *Oh yeah, that's me!*

And then they'll do what's best to make A Few Cool Hardware Stores bigger, stronger, and better positioned to compete in today's retail world and more likely to carry on the legacy that we have built over the last 20 years. I started Logan Hardware all those years ago with an eye toward improving my community, and making life a little better for everyone who lived there. I got so much more than that in the bargain, including amazing teammates who helped members of those communities while they wandered through the plant aisle, or the plumbing aisle, in search of the right tool for the job.

I felt some ghosts in the room that day too. Tommy, Todd, John, Skippy, Jen, Drew. So many hours of people's lives that carried me to where I was standing, and I wished in that moment to see their faces in the gathering as well.

For all the communities and the thousands of customers that have supported us, pushed us, and spent hard earn cash with us, all I can say is *thank you.* I bet most of you have no idea of the small part you played in ensuring that Recovery Hardware was seeded and grew and at some point in time took on a life of its own.

Top 5 100% Employee-Owned Businesses

Depending on what list you look at, there are roughly 6,000 ESOPs in the United States. Despite the incentives to form one, we are all still unique. When Marc and I started down our transition path, we hadn't heard of most of them but are now proud to count ourselves among their ranks. Here are the biggest ones I found in my research:

Penmac/Springfield, MO Agency/28,000 employees	Staffing
WinCo Foods/Boise, ID	Supermarkets/20,700 employees
Amsted Industries/Chicago, IL Components/18,000 employees	Industrial
Brookshire Brothers/Lufkin, TX	Supermarkets/16,000 employees
Houchens Industries/Bowling other/15,600[42] employees Green, KY	Supermarkets and

And for my teammates in recovery who get out of bed each day with a resolve to *be.* To be heathy, to be strong, to be a force in their own lives. Never, ever believe that you are anything less than remarkable. Never doubt that you can do anything you put your mind to, and that the world is a better place with you in it.

I'm so proud that going into our 20th year a brand-new path has been charted for our team. The stories I've told about Shane and Mike and Marcus are just the tip of the iceberg of what any company can do—local or otherwise. I fully expect our legacy to continue in any next chapter written by the new owners of A Few Cool Hardware Stores.

You're a Miracle, John Harden

He wore a black cross-body bag that we affectionately named Paula. Paula was about the size of a large cell phone and "her" purpose was to hold a device that constantly distributed medicine to John's fragile heart and lungs so that they would not fail.

I foolishly thought that by personifying her with a name, a personality, Paula would never stop working and John wouldn't be ashamed of having her strapped to his side everywhere he went. While John's spirit took it in stride, the bag was a constant reminder of his tenuous hold on life. He couldn't give her the night off so he could enjoy a romantic date and she clung annoyingly to his side while he sat at his desk.

John started as a sales associate at Logan Hardware on September 29th of 2014 and I truly think he was sent to make me a better human being. He saw the good in everyone which he reminded me of daily by exclaiming, "You're a miracle, Gina Schaefer!"

I would hear this rave review repeated throughout the day but with other names, like when a cashier would come into his periphery, or the store manager would walk by, and John would call out, "You're a miracle, Tim Hamm!"

No matter who he was yelling about, I would smile behind my computer as if he were talking to me.

When John arrived at Logan Hardware, he was 49 years old and had been clean for about a year.

"How did you find us?" I wanted to know.

"You were all the chatter in the recovery rooms," John told me. I had learned at some point that "room" meant a 12-step meeting and I smiled at being worthy of conversation in those crucial circles. John told me that he was "beaten down with no self-esteem or purpose"—his vocabulary steeped with the heavy words echoed often by my teammates: *lost, sad, alone, depressed* and *broken*. There is lots to be read about the opposite of addiction being connection and John needed a connection in a really big way. Fortunately for all of us, he found it with us at Logan Hardware.

John told me he was sure that no one would hire him. But one day, while walking past our new location he got a feeling *that Logan Hardware would be his way out*—a guardian angel in the form of bricks and bolts and shopping carts. For some reason walking by our "shiny new hardware store" made John think he had a chance at a shiny new life too.

Later in our conversations, John explained a saying that goes something like "social acceptability does not equal recovery," but he did need a confidence boost and he thought that by getting a job at Logan Hardware he might just end up clean, employed, and accepted. I still shake my head hearing his voice say these words. John was loved by so many people. He was *social and acceptable* in the best possible ways, and it breaks my heart to think he didn't always recognize that.

John was born and raised in Alabama in a family that valued hard work. His dad and brother were proud union men and John grew up learning to do everything associated with fixing a house. These lessons served him well when he and his long-time partner bought a fixer upper in Dupont Circle just west of Logan Circle. During that lifetime (I swear John had 10 lives), he worked for United Airlines, finished home improvement projects and lived what seemed to be his best life.

That life was shattered though when his partner died, and John, convinced that he was going to die too, moved back to Alabama and slowly succumbed to drug addiction. Although he can easily be described as one of the kindest people who has worked for us, like many of my teammates in recovery, it is incredibly hard to imagine John off the grid with a needle in his arm. Yet that is how he lived between 2007 and 2014.

It has occurred to me on more than one occasion that many of my teammates are survivors of the fallout from the AIDS epidemic. They may have lived through it, and are grateful for that, but they paid a heavy price. Their penalty for survival was watching friends, lovers and neighbors die in droves, sending them into a tailspin that included depression and self-medication and addiction. I knew a thing or two about fallout; I wasn't in Logan Circle during the riots, but I saw the aftermath, the sadness and decay left in their wake. In addition to helping pick up the pieces from that long, drawn-out void, I wanted to create a space for the teammates who had their own pasts to grapple with. Maybe this is what John felt on that fateful day he walked into our lives.

John very vividly remembered walking into the store for his group interview. "A Hispanic contractor opened the door for me and wished me luck," he told me. "I took that as a friendly omen, Gina."

John told the five people in the interview who he was, why he was there and that he was looking for a second chance. He was hired and started working almost immediately—but not before making sure that Sundays were a non-negotiable day off for church. A proud and very active member of Foundry United Methodist Church, John found his true calling in the choir and as an activist—supporting the Church's quest for full inclusion of LGBTQ+ persons in the life and ministry of the parish.

Years later, he told me how the sun was shining brightly on his first day—a beautiful early fall afternoon and again, how it felt like fate was smiling on him.

One of our company's core values is "Always Grow and Share" and John lived up to this for sure. He taught anyone and everyone around him willing to listen and learn. The garden department became his pulpit and our teammates his followers. He turned 50 in that store—surrounded by co-workers who adored him and customers who sought him out for advice and counsel or just a friendly smile. "That milestone was made even more memorable," he told me, *"Because I remembered it*—clean and sober." Exactly how he wanted to be.

Eventually, John became too sick to work on the sales floor, Paula wasn't strong enough to do her job effectively, but we weren't ready to let him go. After reducing his hours as much as he could, he found himself installed as my new Executive Assistant and Community Outreach Liaison. John gave himself the second part of that title because he personally "wanted to be sure we were doing all we could to help the community as much as the DIYers." I was all for it—and who was going to argue with John?

For 22 months, he occupied the desk immediately outside of my office. It had a big sunny window with a view of 14th Street and he decorated it with plants and poems and customer comments that made him smile. We would yell back and forth to each other, make jokes, and just generally keep each other motivated. My day didn't seem to start until he'd walk by my door on his way to that desk, usually around 10 a.m. every morning. When he wasn't around, I was acutely aware of his absence partially because I knew that someday it would be permanent.

It didn't take long for John to slot himself in as my boss. Perhaps because he had nothing to lose, but he more than anyone else felt free to give me advice and offer constructive criticism. Suggestions for how to do something better, for how to *be better*. No one else treated me this way and I loved him for it.

At the same time, John was incredibly fragile. With each passing week he began coming to work more and more slowly and eventually a nurse was assigned to visit him at the office. Each time the nurse arrived with a warm smile for John, I'd whisper a little prayer that he had brought some miracle along in his medical bag. I hoped that somehow, when he left, John would be cured, and we would never have to see the nurse again, even though he was only there to ensure Paula had what she needed to keep pumping. There was no miracle inside that bag.

Two things I know for sure, John was a showman at heart, and he wanted people to lighten up and embrace their sense of fun. Each year, during summertime holiday weekends, DC becomes a ghost town as thousands of beachgoers head to the shores of Maryland and Delaware. Traffic in town all but disappears and the waft of suntan lotion can be smelled 90 miles away. Everyone rents houses or stays with friends and parties their asses off until it is time to go home.

If bottomless mimosas and minty mojitos are your jam, you're in for a treat. But John and Shane and their sober friends didn't want to miss out on beach fun. They just recognized that it might need to look a little differently for them, so they started an annual drag show called Miss Summer Serenity. The event functions as a fundraiser for the Triangle Club, which serves the LGBTQ+ recovery community, but more importantly, gives them all a fun and clean event at the beach—and there is nothing serene about it!

The Recovery Hardware Playlist

I quizzed my more musically inclined friends for songs that reference hardware or tools and got back more answers than I have room for. Who knew that my industry provides such rich material to croon about?

- "If I Had a Hammer," by Peter, Paul and Mary
- "Birdhouse in Your Soul," by They Might Be Giants
- "El Condor Pasa (If I Could)," by Simon & Garfunkel
- "Sixteen Tons," by Tennessee Ernie Ford
- "Scarlet Begonias" by the Grateful Dead
- "Screwdriver" by Prince
- "Hardware Store" by Weird Al Yankovic
- The Bob the Builder Theme Song
- Anything by MC Hammer
- "Fix you" by Coldplay
- "Sledgehammer" by Peter Gabriel

In 2019, Summer Serenity was held at a nearby theater in the city instead of at the beach, so Marc and I had a chance to attend. John was MC that year and he took his role VERY seriously. He had multiple costume changes that even included a bright yellow tuxedo jacket complete with tails and feathers. He did a solo number halfway through the competition which I have no doubt he made non-negotiable when he took the job.

Our teammate Carl competed on center stage and he absolutely glowed under the spotlight. He'll tell you he was sparkling because he was sweating his ass off in his spandex get up, but

I know it was because he was caught up in the attention. He was shining from the inside out. He shimmied and shook his way through Patti LaBelle's "I Believe" in four-inch heels and a skintight sequined leotard. The lyrics touched our hearts and the whole audience swayed and sang along as if he was the queen himself–the poignancy lost in the thrill of the performance:

There are miracles in life I must achieve
But first I know it starts inside of me, oh
If I can see it then I can be it
If I just believe it, there's nothing to it
I believe I can fly

Carl had an outsized afro perched on his head that shook along with his booty and all I could think was: *If the old hardware guys could see us now!* The theater was fairly small. I guesstimate there were about 200 attendees and most of them were gay men from the local recovery community. As the curtain closed and the event sponsors were thanked, the MC added one final special message to send the patrons out the door.

"I know I don't speak alone when I say that many in this room owe our sobriety to Logan Hardware," he said looking at us with a smile. "Please join me in a round of applause for Marc Friedman and Gina Schaefer, who are sitting in row 3." My heart leapt and I heard Marc gasp next to me. John had found a way to cast the warm sunlight that seemed to follow him out into the bleachers to rest on our shoulders and it felt incredible.

John often said he had never met anyone who did the right thing so naturally but one day I needed a big nudge. We were on a trip to Baltimore, and John told me that I should write this book.

I had always felt as though the stories of our teammates were not mine to tell. It was as if by talking about this person's addiction or that one's recovery efforts, I would be sharing secrets best left under wraps. As if just maybe, if these stories remained secrets, they would go away for those who had lived them. Not because I was ashamed of them, in fact I was proud as hell.

But when I explained this to John, he turned around in his seat and said pointedly, "If you don't talk about the folks we hire and tell their stories, Gina, who will?" John, who believed that everyone he met was a miracle, was passing the torch to me.

The day John died was the saddest day of my life. When I got the call, I was on a train to New York City to see *Hamilton* on Broadway with Marc and some dear friends. The scenery flashed by as the train sped farther and farther from the city and the more DC receded, the more relaxed we all became. We were buoyant in our escape and a beautiful sunny winter day mirrored our moods. I knew when I had kissed him goodbye the day before that it would be the last time I saw John, but that didn't lessen the blow. I was desperate to hold on to him but knew it was time for him to go. His faith was strong, and he was ready for his next stage. He made me promise I would write this book, and that I would speak at his celebration service—he would be the man of the hour, yet he gave me the last word.

Heartware Stories

As a lead up to its 100th anniversary, Ace sent a professional film crew around the country to document the heartstring pulling stories that its members bring to life in their own communities. If there is a dry eye after watching most of these videos, something is wrong with the viewer. To me, these stories bring Main Street to life. They highlight the power of small businesses to impact their communities.

My friend Adam Keith, a third-generation Ace retailer, started raising and training service dogs after meeting a veteran suffering from PTSD. Adam's dad was one of the first Ace retailers I met in 2002. He was welcoming and tried to share as much knowledge as he could in the four short days we were together. It is no surprise that he has raised such a compassionate son.

Find the Ace Hardware story, A Puppy Named Freedom on YouTube

A tragic accident took the life of a young sales associate who worked with my buddies at Whitmore Ace in Illinois. In 2010, they began an annual tradition of collecting prom dresses so girls in their community, regardless of financial ability, can be the belle of the ball. Each prom season, an average of 2000 dresses are given away and the event grows more popular each year.

Find the Ace Hardware story, Melissa's Closet on YouTube

In 2019, we were asked to tell the story of Recovery Hardware and I watched as our storytelling became breathtaking.

The film crew arrived at Logan Hardware on a pretty Sunday afternoon and after documenting my side of the story, they got to work on the real magic sauce—my team. If you were on the team, in recovery, and willing to talk about it that camera found its way into your face. John didn't want the spotlight but had helped select the teammates who should be interviewed then he and I sat in the back of the room like set moms, calling out encouragements and cracking jokes to put our actors at ease. It was one of my proudest moments as a business owner.

Find the Ace Hardware story, Second Chances on YouTube

Acknowledgments

T his book came to life because two very special teammates planted the seeds. To Mark Wasson, who told me that our store had become known as Recovery Hardware in the neighborhood—thank you, Mark, for opening my eyes to this, and so many other things besides. If you hadn't found your way to the front door at Logan Hardware all those years ago, our lives would be very different.

A very special thanks to the miracle John Harden, who left us far too soon—his assertion that "someone needs to tell these stories and that somebody should be you, Gina!" is what made me put pen to paper. I miss you every day.

Thank you to several special friends who read chapters, questioned word choices, and supported various parts of the project in ways that lifted my spirit over the years that it has taken to complete: Jeannie Esti, Andrea Viera, Megan Bauman Lewis and so many others shared their time with me right when I needed it most.

To Ace Hardware—a cooperative like no other. What started auspiciously has become a partnership of mutual respect and one that has enabled my business to grow with no boundaries. Thank you for building such a strong network of support for dreamers like me.

I am deeply indebted to my high school pal and wordsmithing genius, Cheryl Laughlin, whose uncanny ability to talk me off the ledge with chats about growing up in Ohio or about designer combat boots ensured that I kept going—smiling and even laughing through this process.

To my incredible editor, Beverly West, who stewarded me from a rough draft to something I am really proud of—I am so grateful to have shared this experience with you. You've taught me so much about the world of book writing, how to have fun, how to tell a story professionally, and how to craft the perfect through line. I am forever grateful to you.

I am so appreciative of my parents who encouraged entrepreneurialism and hard work from a young age. They planted the seed in me that girls can do anything—including running hardware stores!

I wish I knew how to truly summarize all that my husband, business partner and all-around best friend and life teammate has meant to me in this process. I have no doubt that my questions, stress and excitement caused some of his own. Thank you, Marc Friedman, I love you.

No small business thrives without its customers. We've had millions over the years and hope that we continue to live up to your expectations. You make us want to be better community members every day, and we are successful only because you walk through our doors.

And finally, to my teammates. You are the real reason I get out of bed every day, fight the competition and try to make us better at what we do. Each and every one of you is amazing in your own special way. For those of you in recovery, I applaud your efforts and please know you have a special place at this company now, in our history and in the years to come.

Resources

If you or someone you care about needs help, considering starting with one of the resources listed here.

Alcohol and Drug Abuse Helpline
1-800-234-0420

Alcoholics Anonymous
aa.org

Narcotics Anonymous
Na.org

Chrystal Meth Anonymous
Chrystalmeth.org
855-638-4373

Endnotes

1   Marisa M. Kashino, "The Reinvention of 14th Street: A History," Washingtonian, April 4, 2018, https://www.washingtonian. com/2018/04/04/how-14th-street-came-back-reinvention-a-history/.

2   "The Four Days in 1968 That Reshaped D.C.," the Washington Post, March 27, 2018, https://www.washingtonpost.com/graphics/2018/local/ dc-riots-1968/.

3   "An Anatomy of the Riots," the Washington Post, April 4, 1988, https:// www.washingtonpost.com/archive/politics/1988/04/03/an-anatomy-of-the-riots/a78560fe-bbfc-4572-8db9-a4c50a06f58d/.

4   Patrice Gaines-Carter, "For Riot Victims' Kin, The Pain Endures," the Washington Post, April 5, 1988, https://www.washingtonpost.com/ archive/politics/1988/04/05/for-riot-victims-kin-the-pain-endures/ fff53dc7-5435-49d4-8782-0effa160b1c9/.

5   Michael E. Rune, "Fifty years ago some called D.C. 'the colored man's paradise.' Then paradise erupted," the Washington Post, March 26, 2018, https://www.washingtonpost.com/local/fifty-years-ago-some-called-dc-the-colored-mans-paradise-then-paradise-erupted/2018/03/22/6ae9ec1c-208e-11e8-94da-ebf9d112159c_story.html.

6   "About Ace Hardware," ACE, accessed February 1, 2022, https://www. acehardware.com/about-us.

7   "Ace Hardware giving away 1 million flags at stores on May 23," WRAL. com, updated May 23, 2020, https://www.wral.com/ace-hardware-giving-away-1-million-flags-at-stores-on-may-23/19111085/.

8   "Cooperative identity, values & principles," International Cooperative
    Alliance, accessed February 1, 2022, https://www.ica.coop/en/
    cooperatives/cooperative-identity.

9   "Explore Washington, D.C.'s Historic Black Broadway on U Street,"
    National Trust for Historic Preservation, accessed January 31, 2022,
    https://savingplaces.org/guides/explore-washington-dc-black-broadway#.
    YfiSS1jMJfU.

10 "Explore Washington, D.C.'s Historic Black Broadway on U Street."

11 "Black Broadway, Madame Lillian Evanti and D.C.'s Black History,"
    the Washington Informer, February 15, 2021, https://www.
    washingtoninformer.com/black-broadway-madame-lillian-evanti-and-d-c-
    s-black-history/.

12 "Our Founder: Father Greg," Homeboy Industries, accessed February 1,
    2022, https://homeboyindustries.org/our-story/father-greg/.

13 Martin Wolk, "Father Gregory Boyle has an ambitious plan to expand
    Homeboy industries," the Los Angeles Times, December 5, 2019, https://
    www.latimes.com/entertainment-arts/books/story/2019-12-05/gregory-
    boyle-barking-to-the-choir-book-club.

14 Yian Q. Mui, "Longed-For Store Arrives in Tenleytown Ace Hardware
    Fills Hechinger's Void," the Washington Post, June 19, 2006, https://
    www.washingtonpost.com/archive/business/2006/06/19/longed-for-store-
    arrives-in-tenleytown-span-classbankheadace-hardware-fills-hechingers-
    voidspan/897d24f0-6630-4d30-bcad-f8f6e0a97f0f/.

15 "Washington DC History Resources," accessed February 1, 2022, https://
    matthewbgilmore.wordpress.com/district-of-columbia-population-
    history/.

16 Paulo Coehlo, The Alchemist (New York: HarperCollins, 2015).

17 "Our Roots," Cole Hardware, accessed February 1, 2022, https://www.
    colehardware.com/about-us/#:~:text=Cole%20Hardware%20has%20
    been%20around,purchased%20the%20store%20in%201959.

18 Edward M. Brecher, Licit & Illicit Drugs: The Consumer Union Report
    on Narcotics, Stimulants, Depressants, Inhalants, Hallucinogens, and
    Marijuana – Including Caffeine, Nicotine, and Alcohol (Yonkers, NY:
    Consumer Reports, 1927).

19 "The History of Baltimore," Baltimore City, accessed February 1, 2022, http://www.baltimorecity.gov/sites/default/files/5_History.pdf.

20 Ron Cassie, "City of Immigrants," Baltimore, accessed February 1, 2022, https://www.baltimoremagazine.com/section/historypolitics/city-of-immigrants-the-people-who-built-baltimore/.

21 "The History of Baltimore."

22 Lori Sears, "At its centennial, revisit Great Fire and its aftermath," the Baltimore Sun, February 5, 2004, https://www.baltimoresun.com/bal-li.family05feb05-story.html.

23 Ibid.

24 Paul Jackson, "U.S. Foreclosure Filings Up 42 Percent in 2006," Housing Wire, January 25, 2007, https://www.housingwire.com/articles/us-foreclosure-filings-42-percent-2006/.

25 "Baltimore, Maryland Population History," Biggest US Cities, accessed February 1, 2022, https://www.biggestuscities.com/city/baltimore-maryland.

26 "Federal Hill Demographics," Point2, accessed February 1, 2022, https://www.point2homes.com/US/Neighborhood/MD/Baltimore-City/Federal-Hill-Demographics.html.

27 Richard Gorelick, "Michael Phelps' old breakfast stop serves up Olympic-sized lunch," the Baltimore Sun, July 29, 2012, https://www.baltimoresun.com/food-drink/bs-ae-phelps-petes-grille-20120729-story.html.

28 Brenna Williams, "Jada Pinkett Smith Talks Growing Up in Baltimore," Huff Post, August 4, 2015, https://www.huffpost.com/entry/jada-pinkett-smith-talks-growing-up-in-baltimore-thankful-for-the-hollywood-scrutiny_n_55bfc088e4b06363d5a2fc25.

29 "About," Things by HC, accessed February 1, 2022, https://thingsbyhc.com/pages/about-us.

30 Terry Gross, "'Cities Are Resilient,' Says Baltimore Crime Novelist Laura Lippman," NPR, July 30, 2019, https://www.npr.org/2019/07/30/746433092/cities-are-resilient-says-baltimore-crime-novelist-laura-lippman.

31 "The 3 best plant nurseries in Baltimore," Hoodline, April 28, 2020, https://hoodline.com/2020/04/the-3-best-plant-nurseries-in-baltimore/.

32 Buddy T., "How Long Does Methamphetamine (Meth) Stay in Your System?" Verywell Mind, updated November 28, 2021, https://www.verywellmind.com/how-long-does-methamphetamine-stay-in-your-system-80283.

33 Sarah Hardey, ed., "How Long Does Meth Stay in Your System?" American Addiction Centers, updated Janaary 31, 2022, https://americanaddictioncenters.org/meth-treatment/how-long-in-system.

34 T., "How Long Does Methamphetamine (Meth) Stay in Your System?"

35 "John Weintraub and Ed Copenhaver," Capitol Hill History Project, March 19, 2002, https://drive.google.com/file/d/1cqEX7_oLfHpeDXsGLW694u8ZkabnLK3m/view.

36 "#246: What does it take to for a company to survive for 100 years…" Intentional Growth podcast, April 28, 2021, 64 mins.

37 "The AFCARS Report," Children's Bureau, June 23, 2020, https://www.acf.hhs.gov/sites/default/files/documents/cb/afcarsreport27.pdf.

38 "About the children," AdoptUSKids, accessed January 31, 2022, https://www.adoptuskids.org/meet-the-children/children-in-foster-care/about-the-children.

39 "6 Quick Statistics On The Current State of Foster Care," iFoster, November 9, 2020, https://www.ifoster.org/blogs/6-quick-statistics-on-the-current-state-of-foster-care/.

40 "What Are the Dangers of Aging Out of Foster Care?" Adoption.org, December 12, 2019, https://adoption.org/dangers-aging-foster-care.

41 "Midwest Evaluation of the Adult Functioning of Former Foster Youth: Outcomes at Age 26," Chapin Hall at the University of Chicago, 2011, https://www.chapinhall.org/wp-content/uploads/Midwest-Eval-Outcomes-at-Age-26.pdf.

42 "List of ESOP Companies," National Center for Employee Ownership, accessed February 3, 2022, https://www.nceo.org/employee-ownership-data/esop-company-lists.

CPSIA information can be obtained
at www.ICGtesting.com
Printed in the USA
BVHW031800010922
646073BV00025B/380